ARE RELATED?

How to find your famous ancestors

Eve McLaughlin

Illustrations by Nick Newman

COUNTRYSIDE BOOKS

First Published 2002
© Eve McLaughlin 2002

COUNTRYSIDE BOOKS
3 Catherine Road
Newbury, Berkshire

To view our complete range of books,
please visit us at
www.countrysidebooks.co.uk

ISBN 1 85306 741 5

Produced through MRM Associates Ltd., Reading
Designed by kdp, Kingsclere
Printed by Woolnough Bookbinding Ltd, Irthlingborough

Contents

ARE WE RELATED?

CHAPTER 1

ARE WE RELATED?

It is a natural instinct to want to be related to someone famous, so that you can point to the history books and say: 'Look, that's my six times great-grandfather's brother's great-grandson.' Which is fine, if you have worked out the connection in detail and can produce an outline pedigree to show the unbelievers. But what happens if you have no proof, other than a vague family rumour? How can you assess the probabilities and find out if it is true? Far too many people *want* to be related, so they move on from wanting to saying: 'maybe we are related', and from 'maybe' to 'of course we are' – and their families naturally believe it is true.

Is it likely to be true?

First, you need to take a long, hard look at the source of that rumour. Who told you? Uncle Joe, who seems vaguely ashamed that his decent, godfearing ancestors could ever be linked with profligate aristocracy? Or Auntie Maybelle, who spends her life reading romantic novels and swooning over pictures of the royal family? And where did they get the story from? Uncle Joe may have heard it from his grandmother, as great a novel-reader in her time as Maybelle, or who didn't actually know, but had been snooping on grown-up conversation one day and took a story about titled people to be about the family.

Think about the age of the informant when the persons concerned were alive. Could they have had the story directly from the horse's mouth, as it were? If the person involved was dead a hundred years before your informant was even alive, then who told him or her? Even if there is a slight overlap, is it likely that the person would have been chatting to your own informant on a confidential level? A five-year-old probably won't have been the bosom friend of a septuagenarian, though raise the age to the teenage years and the possibility is there.

Small children do listen with great avidity to the conversation of their elders, but they often filter information through a dim haze of incomprehension and get the wrong idea. I know a lady who was convinced her great-grandfather was a big hog-rancher. Her mother told her so, and Mother never told a lie. And there was a precise quotation, remembered through the years, which 'proved' it. It turned out that he was a farm labourer who had married the widowed landlady of the Pig and Whistle inn. So his oft-quoted statement that 'I keeps the Pig and the Pig keeps me' was absolutely correct, though hardly tactful.

There are also cases where a family tradition has a basis in truth, but has been affixed to the wrong generation. A story might be passed down the chain of communication in your family until your great-aunt tells you it about 'Grandfather'; but she means her grandfather, not yours. A couple of repetitions of that, and the 'fact' may apply to six or seven generations back.

A very truthful old lady told me that her grandfather X used to clack away on his loom on Sundays, to annoy the people in the church across the road. Her nonconformist father had told her, proudly. But that side of the family had only moved to their house near the church two generations back, his father and grandfather were carpenters and builders and earlier farmers, and not one of the X family were ever weavers. Indeed, hand loom weaving had ended in the village with the Industrial Revolution by about 1790. The information turned out to be true, but applied to a maternal ancestor who died, a weaver and an unrepentant dissenter from the church, in 1770. The sturdy resistance to church authority had made an impression and was repeated down the generations to show what could be done. Two hundred years later, Miss X told me.

It says it on the IGI so it must be true

There was definitely an impression in Victorian and later times that all people with the same name were related. You can see the effect in the International Genealogical Index. This was originally created for religious purposes, since members of the Church of Jesus Christ of Latter-day Saints (LDS) were supposed to find out and baptise their ancestors, and this was extended in the early days to all 'kinsfolk'. Individuals had to assemble this information as best they could, by personal visits to the homeland or by using record agents to collect data. The individuals were then responsible for baptising the ancestors by proxy. No one questioned that the information, gathered and submitted in good faith, was true, though very often it was faultily transcribed or insufficiently thoroughly checked.

Later, to enable easier research and some checking to be done, a programme of systematic filming and indexing of parish registers was undertaken in all countries from which LDS members had come, especially the UK, Germany and the Scandinavian countries. In the UK certainly, this did not include every register by any means, since permission was sometimes refused, generally by the Bishop of that diocese or for an individual parish by some of the clergy.

Burials are not normally included in the IGI, for religious reasons, other than as a note against a handful of names that the baptised child died under eight. This is not the result of systematic research and matching of data, but just a note where the information is to be found adjacent to the baptismal entry and can be readily paired with it. If a child died aged nine or so, there is no annotation, though this invalidates him or her as an ancestor. These two reasons make it unsafe to put together even the skeleton of a pedigree from the IGI alone, because all the basic facts are not there. It is a useful lead towards further research and proper checking in the original records.

But there is more. The indexed entries and personally collected entries were put together into a computer database, the Computer File Index, which was later renamed the International Genealogical Index. This means that the source of entries may be either the 'controlled extraction' made by staff employed to make the Index, or names submitted, maybe years before, and never checked for accuracy. The latest version of the IGI includes many entries from old records of names collected in the 1920s or so by church members who had not identified the entries but assumed that, because the name was the same as theirs or their mother's, they were 'relatives'. Some even invented dates and places to make the entry look more plausible. These 'relative' entries are often a long way from authentic, but if the stated inputter was a likely relation, then the temptation is to claim the entered person as well.

Worse still is Ancestral File, a collection of pedigrees created by individuals, some after good research but too many on incomplete or downright sloppy work. They are submitted to the LDS and reproduced without further checks. Unfortunately, the IGI and Ancestral File are not clearly distinguished, especially if accessed through the on-line Family Search, and many people have been led to believe that they are accurate information.

Check carefully anyway

So if your 'family tradition' is based on what you or a relative found in the IGI or, worse, in Ancestral File, then you would be wise to forget it and start afresh, or note it, but check every step of the way. In particular if you are relying on one of these vague claims or family rumours to show a connection to a member of the peerage, do think twice and search very carefully for genuine evidence before confronting some bemused peer as 'Cousin George'!

CHAPTER 2

L.J.SILVER

THE NAME'S THE SAME

Sometimes the source of the whole rumour is that your family name is the same as that of a noble or gentry family. A great deal depends on what *kind* of name it is. The vast majority of names are not unique to one family, or even to one location. The first thing to consider is if the name is likely to have multiple origins.

Surnames come from four basic sources:

1. They can be **OCCUPATIONAL**. This means that there are any number of unrelated people called Carpenter, Butcher, Baker, Dyer, Cartwright, Miller, Smith, as well as the obsolete trades like Fletcher (arrow-cutter), Pargeter (fancy plasterer), Stringer (of bows), Girdler (belt-maker), Lorimer (spur-maker) or Wright (-maker).

2. They can be **PATRONYMIC**. Take a standard forename and add 'son', or 's'; take the various diminutives of the name, add double diminutives (like 'ett', 'att', 'ell', 'let', 'lin', 'kin', 'ling', 'cock') and do the same.

For **Richard** this gives you: Richardson, Richards, Richason, Rich, Rickard, Ricketts, Rixon, Ritchie, Richens, Dickson, Dix, Dickerson, Dickens, Dickinson, Dickie, Diggs, Diggens, Hickson, Hix, Hickin, Hitchens, Higgs, Higgison, Higgins, Higgett, Hitchcock, Hiccock and many more.

William gives Williams(on), Wills, Wilson, Willis, Willet, Willey, Wilmin, Wilmot, Willock, Wilcock, Wilman; and from the French form **Guillaume**: Gillam, Gilham, Gilmin, Guillemin, etc.

ARE WE RELATED?

Robert has pet names in Rob (Robson, Robbins), Rab (Rabson, Rabbett), Hob (Hobson, Hobbins, Hoblin), Hop (Hopson, Hoppett, Hopkins), Dob (Dobson, Dobbs, Dobbin), Dab (Dabson, Dabbinett, Dapson), Nob (Nobbs, Noblett) and combinations like Dunbobbin, Dunbavin (dark little Robert) or Rabjohn (Robert John).

Thomas has all the forms beginning with Thom- or Tom, Tomlins, Tompkins, Thomkis, Tamson, Tombleson, and in the north, Tolson, Towlson.

Roger has the obvious forms, then those from the pet name Dodge (Dodds, Dodson, Dodgin), Hodge (Hodgson, Hodson, Hodgkiss, Hotchkins).

Nicholas produces all the variations on Nicholls, Nickolds, Nixon, Nicklin, and from the pet name, Coll, Colin (Collins, Collett, Collis, Colley, etc.) and the Scots McNichol, McColl.

Hugh can appear as Hughes or Hewson, Hewitt, Hewletson, Hewlett, Howlett, Howison, Huitson, Hudd, Hudson, Hutson, Huggett, Huggins, Hullett, Hutchens, Hutchinson, Hutcheon, Howchin, etc.

Henry was normally Harry, hence a mass of Harrises, Harrisons, and a few Harrods and Hawkins (though further north you get Hendry and Henderson).

John (apart from Johnson) had a Flemish form of Jan (Janson, Jenkins, Jennings) and Han (Hanks, Hancock) and is very often found in the Welsh derived forms, Jones, Evans. Jack, though everyone thinks of it as the pet form of John (Jackson, Jackett, Jakes, Jackman) could have come equally well from James, which in French is **Jacques**.

Lawrence appears also as Lorrison, Lowrie, Lowson, Lawrie, Larkin, Lawson, Lawkings, etc.

David can be Davis, Davison, Davy, Davitt, Dawson, Dawkes, Dawkins, Dowling, etc.

Philip produces Phipps, Fipps, Phelps, Filson, Pippett, Philcox, Philpot, Potts.

Gilbert gives Gibson, Gibbs, Gibbard, Gillison, Gillett, Giblin, Fitzgilbert (son of).

Peter was normally Per, hence Pears, Pearson, Perkins, Perrett, Parrott.

Matthew not only gives Matson, Matthis, Matteson, but Mayhew and Meacock.

The less common names have fewer pet names and diminutives. **Luke** produces Luckett and Lukins. **Ralph** gives rise to Relphs, Rawlings or Rollins, Rawson, Raffell.

Walter produces Waters, Watts, Watson, Wattis, Watkinson, Watkiss.

Steven produces Stephenson, Steffens, Stimson, Stinson, Stennett.

Adam has Adamson, Addison, Adcock, Adnett, Adin, Adey, Atkins, Aitchison.

Some more rarely used forenames were very popular once, as is shown by the surnames drawn from them: **Bartholomew's** pet name was Bart, Batt or Bate, so you find Bartlett, Bartle, Batson, Bateson, Bateman, Batman (his servant).

Other rare forenames include: Amory, Avery, Garnett, Warner, Clements (Clementson, Climpson), Lambert (Lampson), Lewis, Eustace, Baldwin, Osborn (Usborne, etc.), Hammond (Hamlin, Hampson), Bertram, Silvester (Sillett, Silvey, Silson), Drury, Dennis (Dennett, Dennison), Ingram, Harvey, Herbert (Herbison), Tibbett, Tebbutt (from Theobald), Sanders (from Alexander), Payne (Pagnel), Jarvis, Jarrett.

3.   They may be names from **LOCATIONS** in a village (Churchill, Townsend, Street, Hill, Brook, At-lee, Ford, South, West, North, East, Highfield). Only when people left their native place were they usually called by the name of that village or town.

4.   The final type of surname is probably the largest class, given originally as a **NICKNAME**: from height – Large (Grant, Long), Small (Short, Pettitt, Court, Bass); fatness (Grace, Kedge, Tubb, Barrell); thinness (Rake, Gaunt, but not Thynne, which is 'of the Inn'); complexion or hair (Brown, Black, Grey, White, Burnell, Rudd, Morris); strength (Armstrong, Bull); or deformity: Hand, Legg, Kennedy (ugly head), Campbell (crooked nose), Cruikshank (crooked leg) Foljambe (weak leg), Bossey (hunchbacked).

You can see that there will never be a single, huge, related family from any of the above names, or anything like them, even if the variant you possess is one of the somewhat less common versions. Showing a link to a specific family with one of these names could be possible. Some researchers do collect every instance of the same surname, wherever it occurs in the country, but even they do not claim there is any link between bearers of the more popular names.

ARE WE RELATED?

It is true that some names which fall into the groups above have produced bearers of the name who became noble families. This is not always the name by which the important members of the family are known to the public. It is a curious fact that most people who are given a title of the rank of baron or above generally choose a place name or an aristocratic sounding name rather than their own. This means that if you are called Devonshire, you are certainly not related to the Duke of Devonshire, though if you are Cavendish, you just might be.

The name is not the same

Oddly enough, if the famous family your relatives claim kin with is one whose name is totally unlike yours, or any maternal name you know in the family, the more likely the story is to be true (with reservations). I have given names of folk who may be connected with Nelson, and this is certainly something which would be mentioned with pride.

If, in that case, a tradition is preserved that you are related to a peerage or gentry family, or a man who made a personal achievement, then probably it did not come from the IGI, where you tend to be looking for known ancestral surnames; and it probably didn't come from reading a newspaper or magazine article about the family. Sometimes the fact of a distant relative being rich or influential has been useful to an ancestor in the past and could be useful again in the future, which is why the information is passed down.

If the connection is said to be with a peerage family, first look at *Burke's Peerage*, which names most daughters and says if they have children or not. If you spot a known family surname, then you should be able to prove a connection.

If not, then you need to trace your own family back carefully (see later) and see it a match comes up.

The most popular names in the book

Some people claim connections to the nobility even if their surname is one of the most popular surnames in the phone book and it is true there are always noble families even with these names.

BROWN

Browne with an 'e', though just an older variant, is reckoned to be classier, and I knew a Mr Heygate-Browne who once wrote off to Lord Oranmore and Browne, claiming kin on strength of the 'e'. The secretary wrote back, pointing out that his lordship's pedigree was there for all to see in *Burke's Peerage*, and it did not include Mr H-B, whose grandfather, born plain Brown anyway, had adopted that surname. There was absolutely no link with the distant Irish forebears of Lord Oranmore, a Browne of Carrabrown Castle in Galway.

As an English Brown, he should have tried the Earl of Kenmare (descended from a Brown of Totteridge, Hertfordshire who made money in Ireland in Elizabeth I's time); or the Marquess of Sligo and Lord Kilmaine, both descended from an anonymous English John Brown who went to Ireland in 1580. He could not have proved a connection, but then, it would be difficult to be sure there wasn't one either. There are several plain gentry Irish Browns but the vast majority, Irish or English, just had dark hair or tanned easily.

SMITH

There are ancestral Smiths who became knights and baronets, but it took a really confident man to call himself plain Sir John Smith. So they mostly adopted middle surnames (from the mother's side) and sometimes hyphenated them: Vassar-Smith, Cusack Smith, Workman Smith, Smith-Marriott. One Essex family, descended from plain John Smith of Saffron Walden, decided their name was better spelled as Smijth, tried Smijth-Wyndham, then settled on Bowyer-Smijth, which they adopted by deed-poll, later reverting to Bowyer-Smyth. Robert Smith, who came from a family of well-to-do bankers in Nottingham, bought himself a peerage, and with it a new name. With a little help from the Heralds of the time, he invented a mythical ancestor who fought with the Black Prince, named Sir John de Carrington, and took the title Lord Carrington. The senior line are confident enough to have long dispensed with the legend, though they use the surname Carrington as well as the title. I heard a distant kinsman reciting the myth as truth only a couple of decades ago. However, two of the Nottingham cousins refused from the first to have anything to do with the myth or titles, proud of the achievements of plain Abel Smith, banker. A grandson scooped the pool by marrying a royal granddaughter, who insisted on being known as Lady May Abel-Smith.

ARE WE RELATED?

Another kinsman of Lord Carrington was Oswald Smith of Blendon Hall, in Kent. His daughter married the Earl of Strathmore and was grandmother of the Queen Mother, Elizabeth Bowes-Lyon.

Fred Smith, a barrister from Birkenhead, Cheshire, had two sons who were great lawyers, one the silver-tongued Frederick Edwin Smith, who restored many a criminal to his friends and relations. He was given a title, and became Earl of Birkenhead. Earls generally get a second, subordinate title, and he chose to be Viscount Furneaux, which was his wife's maiden name. The peerage carries the line no further back than his father, so if you are a Birkenhead Smith, who knows?

Another eminent Smith was W.H., founder of the well-known firm of stationers and magazine sellers; his son, a prominent politician, refused a peerage for himself, but took one for his wife and his heirs, who are Viscounts Hambleden. No background is given for the original William Henry Smith.

The 'Smith of Smiths' however, was Rev. Sydney Smith, whose sharp tongue and agile mind has made him remembered in educated circles for his brilliant wit, long after his death. His cleverness and lack of servility meant that he never advanced far in his chosen profession of the Church, though he was moved from unpromising northern country rectories to better paid and better placed work in the south. Aficionados will be found quoting his aphorisms, such as: 'All my life, I have admired a manly man and worshipped a womanly woman but I never could abide a boily boy.'

I would love to be related to Sydney Smith – and I know a man who is.

TAYLOR

John Taylor acquired a bit of land in Ringmer, Sussex, but the real strides were made when his grandson went off to Ireland, to organise a survey for tax purposes, with Sir William Petty. Petty got the knighthood and his family an earldom (Shelburne) but Taylor picked up a nice estate near Kells. His son went into politics and got a baronetcy and his grandson an earldom (of Bective); one of *his* sons, the strikingly named Clotworthy Taylor, got a barony, as Lord Langford, while his elder brother became Thomas Taylour and Marquess of Headfort. The only interesting thing they did thereafter was that the 4th Marquess married the lovely musical comedy actress, Rosie Boot. But most Taylors owned little more than the stool they sat on, to stitch garments.

W. H. Smith (W. H. Smith Archive)

ARE WE RELATED?

WEST

Thomas, appropriately from Devon, was a favourite of Edward II, though apparently heterosexual. He and his family married modest heiresses, but one of these marriages paid off when the girl's half-brothers died childless and she was the only heir to the ancient barony of de la Warr. The Wests acquired that title and jogged along happily as sometime governors of Virginia and later of New York, giving their name to the state of Delaware, until 1800, when they had a crisis of confidence in their plain name. One adopted the name Cornwallis-West, and his son was notorious as the toy-boy of both Jenny, widow of Lord Randolph Churchill and mother of Winston, and later of the actress, Mrs Patrick Campbell. His sister, Mary Theresa, married a very minor German princeling, and dominated the London scene as Daisy, Princess of Pless. His elder cousin, Earl de la Warr, married a Sackville, and adopted the name Sackville-West and eventually just Sackville. A daughter, Vita (Victoria) Sackville-West, married the author Harold Nicholson and wrote herself, but is perhaps better remembered for her unconventional lifestyle and her achievements as a garden creator, at Sissinghurst Castle in Kent.

BUTLER

Any nobleman, from the king down to barons, had a butler to look after his drinks. It was an excellent position for coming by gifts from grateful (and slightly drunk) guests or family. Butlers to the royal family, over the centuries, received a lot more than the odd cash handout, and were often given lands and heiresses.

Theobald Walter was appointed Chief Butler to the King in Ireland (a ceremonial post unless the king visited), and his descendants became Earls and Dukes of Ormonde, Viscounts Mountgarret, Viscounts Ikerin, Earls of Carrick and Barons of Dunboyne. The coheiress of the 6th Earl of Ormonde married William Boleyn and was grandmother of Anne Boleyn, notorious second queen of Henry VIII, which got her father the title over his older cousin. Her fall ended the fortunes of the Boleyn family and the title reverted to a distant Butler fourth cousin, but the dukedom lapsed when the line ran out of male heirs again, and it took a century for the next male heir to get back the earldom.

All this time, the junior lines of the Butler family continued to produce sons, so the name continued with lesser titles or none. If you have Butlers from Ireland in your family, you just might be able to claim kin, though most gentry

Irish families are well written up, and non-gentry families are very hard indeed to trace, as many records have been lost.

It's a place name, so we must have owned it

It is when you come down to the surnames which are names of villages, in England or France, that the temptation mounts to claim that 'we owned the place'. Normally, a man was not called by the name of a place until he left it. At home, he was Will Tomson, or Will Smith, or Will Redhead. Travel elsewhere and he was 'Will, you know, the one from Sheffield'. And Will Sheffield or Shuffill was how he continued to be known. London, Lundin or Lunnon is a relatively common name – but no one would think the ancestor owned the whole of London, just that he came *from* there. It is rarely productive to assume your ancestors can readily be traced to a place just because they bear its name. The leaving would probably have been in medieval times, when surnames were still in the making.

The use of the names of villages as surnames from migrants may confuse the issue if the surname sounds vaguely French. Some are part of a longer double name. (If you came from Piddle Trenthide, which part would you admit to?)

The locations were there before the Norman barons arrived, with a name descriptive of the position or standing. For instance 'Thorpe' just means a village settlement (like German *Dorf* or Dutch *Dorp*). The one belonging to the Norman lord from Manneville or Magneville was named Thorpe Mandeville. Another lord from Isigny gave his name to Thorpe Disney, with a more northern settlement known as the north town, or Norton Disney as well. Possibly Walt Disney's family, way back, left one of those two places. The Cahines barons added their name to the middle village in north Buckinghamshire they owned, as Middleton Cahines, later Milton Keynes, and a number of people named Keynes or Cains could have come from there.

But the same applies to foreign places. A handful of barons came over with William the Conqueror, bringing with them hundreds of foot soldiers, usually from their native place or close by. When the soldiers settled in England, it was asked where they came from, and that became their name – so perhaps Walt Disney's ancestor was a foot soldier from Isigny. And many French traders or mere opportunists arriving in the train of a princess due to marry the king came over well after the Conquest, seeking to make their fortunes, so even a gentry family cannot be traced beyond 1300 or even 1500 with any certainty.

A great many of those French names got mangled by the simple Saxons, so Tocqueville became Tokfield and Tofield, Blonville sur Mer became Blomfield, Caioullet, Callaway, Monceaux, Monsey or Muncey. On some names, they just gave up, hence the popular surnames of French, Norman, Britton (or Brett). Many names have more than one place of origin and the original locations of even baronial or gentry families can be in doubt. If the gentry cannot be traced with certainty to one Aubigny, Ferrieres, Beaumont or Neuville, how much more doubt about your Daubigny/Dabney, Ferrers, Beement and Neville ancestors (who could have got their names at second-hand from an English village anyway)?

It was not just the foreigners who suffered. Think of how many people (from outlandish places in Britain) have the surnames of Scott, Ireland, Cornwall/Cornish, Devonshire, Dorset, Welsh – when they might have been Auchterarder, Ballygonelly, Bozwarthack, Heanton Punchardon, Toller Porcorum, Llantisiliogogogoch.

CHAPTER 3

HOW TITLES WORK

The highest title in the peerage is that of the **monarch** (king or queen). The eldest son is born Duke of Cornwall immediately, and invested with the title of Prince of Wales later. The monarch, male or female, is also Duke of Lancaster.

The younger sons, born His Royal Highness Prince (name) are usually given a dukedom – York, Gloucester, Kent, Edinburgh, Connaught and Albany have been used; they are known as **royal dukes**. Prince Edward was made an Earl (of Wessex), but will inherit his father's title of Duke of Edinburgh one day.

The eldest daughter of the monarch is created the Princess Royal, and she and the younger daughters would normally take the title of their husband; if he has no title, he is usually given one. When Princess Margaret married the photographer Anthony Armstrong Jones, he was created Earl of Snowdon, and retained that title after his divorce. Princess Anne, an independent character, refused a title for either of her (commoner) husbands, Mark Phillips and Timothy Lawrence. Princess Alexandra became The Hon. Mrs Angus Ogilvy, because her husband was the younger son of the Earl of Airlie.

In previous generations, the husbands of princesses normally would have had their own titles. Princess Mary, daughter of George V, married Viscount Lascelles, heir of the Earl of Harewood. Two of Edward VII's three daughters married, the youngest becoming Queen Maud of Norway. The oldest, Princess Louise, married Alexander Duff, Earl of Fife, who was made up to duke; but they had daughters only. Their elder daughter, unusually, was allowed to inherit as duchess, married her cousin, Prince Arthur, but was childless. The title was inherited by her second sister's son, James Carnegie, the Earl of Southesk.

ARE WE RELATED?

Former princesses of the royal house mostly married German princes or dukes of various grades and took their titles. Queen Victoria's eldest daughter was eventually Empress of Germany and mother of the Kaiser; the younger ones were Princess Christian of Schleswig-Holstein, the Duchess of Argyll and Princess Henry of Battenberg.

Apart from royal dukes there are common or garden **dukes**, graded in order as English dukes, Scottish dukes, dukes of Great Britain and Irish dukes. Dukes of the United Kingdom, created since the union in 1801, come last in order of precedence. Dukes generally have the subsidiary title of Earl of this, Baron of that, some of which minor titles may have been inherited through the female lines, if they married heiresses, as they tended to do. Dukes are addressed as 'Your Grace'; their eldest sons will normally use a courtesy title of their father's, as Earl, and even the eldest grandson may have a spare courtesy title. Younger sons are called Lord Henry (family surname), and daughters Lady Mary (family surname). The daughters retain this title if they marry a man without a higher title, and the sons' wives are known as Lady Henry (surname). The oldest dukedom is that of Norfolk, dating from 1483. The earlier ones all failed in male heirs.

The next level is that of **marquess**, with the same area grading. They are formally addressed as 'My Lord Marquess' but informally as Lord (title) and generally have at least one subsidiary title of earl and possibly a barony. The eldest son uses the father's second title, and the younger ones are called Lord James (surname); the daughters are Lady Jane (surname), as above. The oldest marquessate is that of Winchester (1551).

The next level is the **earl**, who may have a second title as Viscount or Baron something, in which case, the eldest son uses it. Younger sons are called the Hon(ourable) Frederick (surname) but the daughters are Lady Anne (surname). Strictly, an earl should be addressed in writing as 'the Right Hon. the Earl of X' or informally as Lord X. His wife is a Countess, written to as 'the Rt Hon. the Countess of X', but is informally Lady X, not Countess X. The oldest earldom is that of Shrewsbury (1442).

A **viscount** may or may not have a subsidiary title and is also written to formally as 'the Rt Hon. the Viscount Y' and addressed as Lord Y. His son and daughter are the Hon. George, the Hon. Sarah (Z, the surname). If the daughter marries, she becomes the Hon. Mrs Jones. The oldest viscounty is that of Hereford (1550).

Barons, the lowest actual peerage level, are Lord (title) and if this is identical with their surname, it may be qualified by a place name – Lord Russell of Liverpool, Lord St John of Bletsoe. Their sons and daughter are Hon. William, Hon. Elizabeth, as for viscounts. The oldest barony is that of de Ros (1264).

Then there are **baronets,** a title invented by James I as a money-raising scheme. The baronet is called Sir Henry Jackson (Bart. or Bt.) and this title is passed on to the eldest son when he dies. His wife is Lady Jackson (not Lady Mary Jackson) and the children have no distinction to their names. The first baronetcies were created in 1611, and nine of these remain in being with Bacon, de Hoghton and Shelley just a few days older than the rest.

The last titled level is that of **knight,** for example Sir Henry Jackson, Kt. – strictly 'Knight Bachelor', though the majority are married. This indicates that the title dies with him, and his children have no distinguishing name. The wife of a knight is Lady Jackson. The female equivalent of knight is Dame, which is a title given to ladies who have achieved distinction in their own right (the husband does not get a reflected title as Sir anything, nor do the children inherit).

There are more recently **life peers,** who might be in any grade but are usually barons or baronesses. The title dies with them. A handful of men recently who have inherited titles have renounced them for themselves, but the title can pass on to their sons. This is a modern process, only legal since 1961.

Normally, once you are a peer, that title stays with you, even if you are convicted of a crime. (Formerly, even in the case of murder, a peer could ask to be tried in the House of Lords, not the common courts, and if found guilty, beheaded, or at least hanged with a silken rope.)

In medieval times, and as late as the 17th century, a peer caught in treason against his sovereign could be *attainted*, losing all his titles. This would usually affect his heirs too, though if they were considered guiltless, or anyway after a period of years, they might be *restored in blood* if the monarch or government agreed. Sometimes only the lesser titles are restored, sometimes several generations miss out and then the counting starts again as if the earls or whatever in between had used their titles. The same applies where the claim to the title was not clear, or not made by the actual heir. In peerage volumes you will see men referred to as *de iure* (by the law) 10th Baron Soaphe, though they were plain Joe Soap to their contemporaries.

Running out of male heirs

The vast majority of titles granted between 1500 and 1950 are heritable by males only. A handful of really old titles could be inherited by an only daughter, and although these are mainly baronies, they do include the earldom of Erroll, whose holder is hereditary High Constable of Scotland, so that in 1941, the 15-year-old Lady Diana Hay became Countess of Erroll and filled her hereditary place at the coronation ceremony of the Queen in 1952, a rather unmilitant young woman of 26.

If ever a peerage runs out of male heirs and is heritable by females, the succession is only clear if there is one daughter alone. If there is more than one, then the peerage goes into abeyance, waiting till all the descendants of every daughter but one have failed, and then the next heir of that daughter can apply for the title, even if it is 200 years since the last baron died. The House of Lords decides if the applicant is properly entitled to the peerage. This was a pretty powerful incentive in the past to get rid of the younger sisters before they married, either by 'accident' or by putting them in a nunnery. In Victorian times, a slightly more civilised system was adopted, whereby the peers would be asked to terminate the abeyance in favour of one particular heiress – usually the one whose husband had most money or political clout.

If a man who has no sons is given a title, he may arrange at the time to have it pass to a brother or other member of his family named. Earl **Mountbatten**, having daughters only, stipulated a *special remainder* of his title to his elder daughter, Patricia (Lady Brabourne) who is now Countess Mountbatten. He was descended from Henry Maurice, Count of Battenberg, son of the Duke of Hesse and his morganatic (non-noble) wife Julie Hauke, created Countess Battenberg.

Henry was a handsome young man and caught the eye of Victoria's youngest daughter, Princess Beatrice, who married him despite his lack of money and estates (they wrote a song about it: 'We're living with Mother now'.) The sons were created marquesses, of Carisbrooke and Milford Haven, and adopted the name Mountbatten in 1914. Lord Louis Mountbatten was a younger son of Milford Haven, given his own title in 1947. His sister Alice (Princess Andrew of Greece) was the mother of Prince Philip of Greece, who also adopted the name Lieutenant Philip Mountbatten, when he became engaged to the then Princess Elizabeth, and was later created Duke of Edinburgh.

Marriage of the Princess Beatrice to Prince Henry of Battenberg, 1885
(From the Royal Collection)

It was in 1914 that the main royal family, having not seen the need for a surname, as such, before, adopted the name (House of) Windsor, while a younger branch, descended from Prince Adolphus, Duke of Cambridge, took the surname Cambridge (their main titles were Marquess of Cambridge and Earl of Athlone, while their sister married King George V). You will find earlier generations of the royal family in the IGI as e.g. Queen Victoria Hanover, which is silly. The family 'name' was Guelph or Wettin, which they did not use.

For higher peerages, where a daughter is the only heiress yet cannot inherit the title directly, especially if there is no close male heir, it is generally the case that her husband will be granted the title as a new creation.

For instance, the **Percy** family really died out in male line in 1110, but the heiress married Joscelin de Louvain, who took the name Percy, and after a time, he was given the title of Baron Percy. Later, two brothers became Earl of Worcester (extinct) and Earl of Northumberland. The male line failed again in 1667, when the 11th Earl, Joscelin, left a small daughter only. She was married off at eleven to young Lord Ogle, but he died before the marriage got serious, and, still under 15, she was married again to Thomas Thynne of Longleat, who was murdered a few months later. In 1682, now just 15, she was matched with the Duke of Somerset, who was 20, and they had a son in 1684, and three daughters. The son, Algernon, inherited the dukedom of Somerset and was given the new title of 1st Earl of Northumberland, and Baron Warkworth. He had a son who died young and a daughter, Elizabeth, who inherited just the old barony of Percy and married a local man, Sir Hugh Smithson, Baronet. Sir Hugh took the name Percy and was created Duke of Northumberland, Lord Lovaine and Baron of Alnwick; after another failure of males which saw the Percy barony go to the Earl of Atholl, through his mother, the dukedom passed to a younger son, also Earl of Beverley. The family then settled down to produce ample males.

However, way back when Earl Joscelin died in 1667, a strong claim was advanced on behalf of a male descendant, Ralph, heir of a Sir Ingelram Percy born in the early 1500s. This man should have been the next male heir, but the claim was laughed at by the House of Lords, because he was an honest tradesman who supported his family by making trunks, and was thought totally unable to carry the dignity of an earldom. So if you can prove a descent from Percy the Trunk-maker, you won't get the dukedom (created later), or the estates (properly descending in the female line), but your moral rights are considerable and you will not be too welcome at Alnwick Castle.

CHAPTER 4

WE MUST BE NORMAN

Often enough, people assume that their name is Norman because it sounds vaguely French, and that if it is French, their ancestors must be barons. True, a number of Norman barons and knights came over with William the Conqueror, though not nearly as many as later claimed they had and paid the monks to get their names inserted in the Roll of Battle Abbey to 'prove' it. If you want to know how many (or few) can actually prove they were at Hastings, reading Anthony Camp's book, *My Ancestors Came with the Conqueror*, is a useful exercise.

They weren't all barons

Some names which 'look' Norman are not. Deverell is not D'Everell, but is said to be from the name of two linked streams in Wiltshire. De'Ath is Death, from someone with a forbidding face, or who acted Death in a medieval pageant. But even if the name is definitely Norman, or French at least, it doesn't mean it belonged to barons.

DEVEREUX

The Devereux barons took their name from Evreux in Eure. They were barons, and various members of the family became Forester of the Earl of Hereford, married the heiress to the barony of Chartley, and the co-heiress of the Earl of Hereford – after which they became Viscount Hereford, a title still in the family. Sir Walter Devereux, favourite of Elizabeth, became Earl of Essex, but got above himself, rebelled and lost the earldom. The viscounty continued through a cousin. There are perfectly genuine relatives of the family in New Zealand now.

But for every baron who came over, there was a whole troop of soldiers, and it was normal for a lord to bring men from his own manor. They were equally from Evreux, so known to their Norman friends as D'Evreux and to Englishmen as Everis or Everest. So there is a good chance of your having a Norman ancestor, but it does not mean he was a baron.

DARCY

The Darcy name came from Arcy in La Manche, and the family were given land mainly in Lincolnshire. The original barony fell into abeyance between two daughters, but a second barony, of Darcy de Knayth, was created in 1304 and inherited by the Conyers family; another Darcy barony was created and the two combined when the heirs married. The grandson, Conyers Darcy, was promoted to Earl of Holdernesse in 1682, but the 4th Earl left no male heirs and that title became extinct; the older baronies went to his daughter Amelia, who married the 5th Duke of Leeds, which effectively 'hid' the baronies of Conyers and Darcy de Knayth in that title. The 7th Duke of Leeds left no male descendants, so a distant Osborne cousin got that title, but the baronies came out of hiding and went to the 7th Duke's sister's son, Sackville Lane Fox. He left surviving daughters only, and they split the baronies, with Darcy de Knayth going to the younger girl, Violet, who married the Earl of Powis. Her only surviving son, George, Viscount Clive, left a small daughter when he was killed in World War Two, Davina Herbert, who became Baroness Darcy de Knayth, while a Herbert cousin inherited the earldom when her grandfather died. She married the brother of Richard Ingrams (founder of *Private Eye*).

There are many Darcy families descended from earlier generations, for the holders of the second Darcy barony, especially, were a prolific lot, with ten children here and fifteen there.

D'AUBIGNY

The D'Aubigny or De Albini name gained lustre from an early bearer, William 'Brito' d'Albini, who was granted huge estates in gratitude for his loyalty, some of them confiscated from rebel barons. His own immediate line ended with Hugh, and his heiresses, but a junior line, descended from a younger son, Ralph, were the Daubignys of Kingsham in Gloucestershire. Elias D'Aubigny's son Ralph married the co-heiress to the barony of Thweng, but she had one daughter only. His second wife, Alice, daughter of Lord Montacute, had sons and grandsons who were plain knights, but a later Giles Daubeney was made a baron by Henry VII, and his son, the Earl of Bridgewater, died childless. The inheritance went to his sisters, of whom Cecily married John Bourchier, Lord Fitzwarine, who became Earl of Bath, and was shared by three co-heiresses after 1636. The other sister, Anne D'Aubeney, married Alexander Buller of Somerset. There was a male cousin, Giles, who was ancestor of a line of untitled Daubeneys in Wayford, Somerset, and Gorwell, Dorset.

The name can develop as Dabney, Debney or Daveney.

There are names which everyone thinks are 'Norman', but which actually turn up in history later than the Conquest. Later immigrants poured across the Channel, intent on making what they could out of a monarchy with close links to Normandy, Anjou, Provence and Poitou.

DACRE

The first proven Dacre was Sheriff of Cumberland in the 1230s, standing loyally by Henry III in his conflict with the great barons. In 1317 Ralph Dacre married the daughter and eventual heiress of Thomas de Multon, Lord of Gillesland, and acquired great estates. He was summoned to Parliament as Baron Dacre in 1321 in right of his wife, and their male heirs were barons. The 6th Baron died in 1457, with his next heir his granddaughter Joan, who married Sir Richard Fiennes, who had sufficient influence to be summoned as Baron Dacre in her right. However, her uncles, Sir Ralph and then Sir Humphrey Dacre, claimed as male heirs, and after a lawsuit got the old family estate of Gillesland and a new barony of Dacre of Gillesland, though Joan Fiennes inherited a large amount of the estate. Henceforth the two Lords were known as Lord Dacre of the North (Humphrey) and Lord Dacre of the South (Richard).

Richard's son, John, married the co-heiress of Lord Fitzhugh, and their son, Thomas, succeeded his grandfather. His son, Thomas, 9th Lord Dacre of the South, was popular at court, but mischievous, and went poaching his neighbour's woods. One night, a park keeper was killed and Thomas, though he didn't do the deed, was accused and executed in 1541 for the crime (an unusually severe punishment for a young gentleman when the deceased was one of the 'lower orders'). His honours were forfeited for a few years, but his young son, Gregory, was restored when he was adult. Gregory died childless in 1594, and his heir was his sister, Margaret, Mrs Sampson Lennard of Chevening.

ARE WE RELATED?

It was ten years before her claim to the barony was successful, and Margaret lived only six more years to enjoy being a baroness. Her son became 12th Baron Dacre in 1611 and the line continued, with the addition of money and lands from minor heiresses, and they were able to rebuild Chevening rather magnificently. (It is today the official country home of the Foreign Secretary and used for international meetings of ministers.)

A substantial input from a cousin, Edward, Lord Barrett, to a younger son enabled him to buy the manor of Horsford, Norfolk, and this branch of the family adopted the name Barrett Lennard after this.

Meanwhile Dacre of the North lived more quietly, but did add a barony, by marriage to Lord Greystoke's heiress. William Dacre, Lord Greystoke, had four sons, of whom three were attainted and the other well out of favour (as a Catholic). Thomas Dacre died in 1569, leaving one son, who died still under age, and three daughters, co-heiresses, who all married Howards: of these Philip Earl of Arundel got Greystoke, his brother William got Naworth, and Thomas, Lord Howard de Walden got most of the rest. The baronies were in abeyance between the heirs of the first two, the Barons Stourton and Petre, and the Earl of Carlisle. Surprisingly for a Catholic, Charles Howard fought well for Cromwell and was rewarded by a barony as Dacre of Gillesland and Earl of Carlisle – one of the two peerages given by Cromwell which were confirmed by Charles II.

Lord Dacre of the South tried to aquire these estates when the last male heir died, but had no chance against the massed Howards, though he did get the old family land at Dacre itself. The 15th Baron married one of Charles II's bastards by Barbara Palmer, but she left only two surviving daughters, one of whom died without heirs, leaving Anne Lennard, who married her cousin, Richard Barrett-Lennard of Belhouse, Essex, and had a son, Thomas Barrett Lennard, Lord Dacre. Her husband died within a few months of the marriage, having run through much of her money. Lady Dacre and her sister were short of cash – and family sentiment – so sold Chevening to Lord Stanhope and Dacre Castle to Christopher Musgrave.

Anne, Lady Dacre, got married again to Lord Teynham, and had two more sons, of whom the elder was the Hon. Charles Roper. The Lennard son died leaving no surviving children in 1786. Charles Roper had married Gertrude, co-heir of Lord Trevor of Glynde, Sussex, and their son, Trevor Roper, inherited the Dacre title, but died childless in 1784. The heir was his sister, Gertrude Roper, who had married Thomas Brand of The Hoo, in Hertfordshire, and had two sons who followed her in the title.

The marriage to Gertrude Trevor probably didn't look important at the time, but she was descended from 'the Patriot' John Hampden's co-heiress Ruth, whose son became Lord Trevor. That title went to Gertrude's half-uncle, Robert, who became Viscount Hampden, though this title lapsed when his sons died childless in 1824. But when a title was needed for the younger brother of Lord Dacre, Henry Bouverie Brand, who had been Speaker of the House of Commons, an office usually rewarded with a peerage, he was made Viscount Hampden. Shortly afterwards he inherited his brother's title of Lord Dacre as well. The title Viscount Hampden continues in the male line of the family, but the barony of Dacre went to the daughter of the 4th Viscount, Rachel Lady Dacre, who married the playwright (Hon.) William Douglas-Home.

Mary (Fluyder), the widow of Trevor Roper, 18th Lord Dacre, left her own fortune in 1808 not to her sister-in-law, Gertrude Brand (Lady Dacre) but to Cadwallader Roper, a younger son of the other son of Anne, Baroness Dacre. This cousin of her husband's took the name not of Fluyder, but of Trevor, as Trevor-Roper, and a descendant of his fourth son, the historian Hugh Trevor-Roper, took the title of Lord Dacre of Glanton, as a life peer. There may well be other Catholic Dacres of the old line, originating in the north of England.

CURZON

My name is George Nathaniel Curzon
I am a most superior person

So the snobbish undergraduate son of Lord Scarsdale was lampooned in an Oxford University revue. He implied such antiquity to the family, but could not prove a (likely) connection with the Curzons of Locking, Berkshire, minor gentry of medieval times. The first certain ancestor was John Curzon of Kedleston, Derbyshire, sheriff and tax collector in Henry VI's time, who bought a baronetcy from James I (a keen salesman, since he needed the money). Sir Nathaniel married the heiress of William Penn of Penn, Buckinghamshire (no relation to William Penn of Pennsylvania, though he tried to prove it).

ARE WE RELATED?

The son married local heiress Mary, daughter of Sir Ralph Assheton, and their son was elevated to Baron Scarsdale in 1761. The 2nd Baron's grandson, the Rev. Alfred Curzon, succeeded his half-uncle as Lord Scarsdale in 1856. George Nathaniel was his eldest son, who went into politics, became a junior minister and then Viceroy of India from 1898 to 1904. This was a regal position and the government were taking a calculated risk with the appointment, for previous holders had mostly been dukes or earls. Curzon had also married an American 'dollar princess', which a number of titled men had tried as a way of restoring their failing fortunes. Mary Zeigler Leiter's money certainly helped him to live in the magnificent style to which he felt he was entitled. Some of the American wives were unable to settle to the life of the English aristocracy, but Mary Curzon was a huge success, a great Vicereine and loving wife. In 1911 Curzon was made up to Viscount and Earl Curzon, and Baron Ravensdale. As he had daughters only, the barony was specially remaindered to them. After Mary's death, he was promoted Marquess of Curzon and married a second American wife, not so successfully.

His nephew inherited the title of Viscount Scarsdale (males only) and the other titles lapsed, but his elder daughter, Mary Irene, became Baroness Ravensdale. She never married, and her heir was the son of her sister, Cynthia, who married the notorious Fascist leader, Sir Oswald Mosley.

A younger son of the family, Assheton Curzon, grandson of the Penn heiress, was created in 1794 Baron Curzon of Penn, and then in 1802, Viscount Curzon. His son, Penn Assheton Curzon, married Sophia, Lady Howe. Her ancestry was chequered but important. Emmanuel, Lord Scrope of Bolton and Earl of Sunderland, had no children by his wife, so he settled his estates on the four children of his mistress, Martha Jeanes. When the son died, his three sisters became co-heiresses to a substantial amount of property and were named by Charles II as if they were legitimate daughters of an earl. So plain Mrs John Howe became Lady Annabel Howe and her eldest son, Scrope, was given the title of Viscount Howe. Another son married one of Prince Rupert's illegitimate daughters, but got no title with her.

One of Viscount Howe's daughters married the Earl of Pembroke and then the Earl of Peterborough's brother. His son, Emmanuel Scrope Howe, married the daughter of Baron Kielmansegg (and Madam Kielmansegg was George I's mistress, which did no harm). They had five sons and four daughters, of whom the eldest son was a general in the American Wars and the second, Richard, the celebrated admiral, who for his achievements was elevated to Earl Howe. As he had daughters only, he was also given a barony which could be inherited by females. The Barony of Howe of Langar went to his eldest daughter Sophia, who married Penn Curzon; their son, Richard, inherited his grandfather's title of Viscount Curzon in 1820 and was advanced to the Earldom of Howe in 1821. Although the heir was childless, there were eight other sons to keep the succession going, with the odd blip when there were daughters only in direct line. The family home near Penn has at the gate a huge ship's figurehead, thought to represent the great admiral, Earl Howe.

MONTAGU/MONTACUTE

The medieval Earls of Montacute and Salisbury, distinguished soldiers to a man, have no provable connection with the later Montagues, whose earliest ancestors' original name was Ladde of Hanging Houghton, Northamptonshire. They did adopt the surname in the mid 15th century and the old Montacute names like Drogo much later. Sir Edward Montagu became a prominent lawyer and royal justice in Henry VIII's reign, always a profitable business. He was one of the governors of the young Prince Edward in 1546. His grandson, Edward again, was made Lord Montagu of Boughton, and his grandson Duke of Montagu, which line went to an heiress twice in three generations. George, Duke of Montagu's heiress married Henry Scott, 3rd Duke of Buccleuch in Scotland, and their second surviving son was given the barony of Montague, but died leaving a daughter (Countess of Home) only. The barony of Montague of Beaulieu, Hampshire, was re-created for the younger son of the 5th Duke of Buccleuch, The 2nd Baron was almost the last male of his line, until after five daughters, a son was at last born when his father was 60, less than two years before his death. His mother (who remarried to become Mrs Pleydell-Bouverie) ran the estate until the boy grew up. He is well known for establishing a motor car museum at his home, Palace House, Beaulieu, then the world's first motorcycle museum, writing dozens of books about vintage cars, and being a pioneer in the opening of stately homes to tourists.

A younger son of the judge, Henry Montagu, born 1563, welcomed James I to London, and became in 1616 Chief Justice of King's Bench, like his ancestor. He was created Baron Montagu of Kimbolton, Viscount Mandeville and finally in 1626 Earl of Manchester – then little more than a country village in the

ARE WE RELATED?

distant north, which, as far as is known, neither he nor his descendants went near except in passing on the way to a castle in Ireland.

His son was resolutely on the Parliamentary side in the Civil War, but refused to sanction the execution of the king, retiring from Parliament until 1660, when he welcomed the restored Charles II. By the first two of his five wives he had seven sons and four daughters. His heir was Robert, 3rd Earl, whose son Charles was one of the first to welcome William III (conforming to family pattern), served as Ambassador to France and a principal Secretary of State, but received no further enhancement until George I's time, when – you've guessed – welcoming the new king, he was elevated to Duke of Manchester.

The family made curiously low-key marriages – only two to daughters of other dukes, and not first-rank dukes at that. Then the 7th Duke burst out and married Countess Luise von Alten, already with a racy reputation, who gave him three children, then remarried at the age of 60 the confirmed bachelor Duke of Devonshire, running a social salon as 'the Double Duchess'. The son, as Viscount Mandeville, went 'shopping' to New York and married rich, Cuban-descended Consuelo Yznaga, whom he made thoroughly unhappy. Not content with this, the next Duke married another dollar princess, Helena Zimmerman.

The younger brother of the first Earl of Manchester, Sir Sidney Montagu, bravely, if wrong-headedly, refused to join the lords of Parliament in opposing the king's excesses in 1641 and was imprisoned in the Tower, but lived to marry Paulina, cousin of Samuel Pepys the diarist. His son, Edward Montagu, did fight on the Parliamentary side and became joint Lord High Admiral, but was

The Earl of Sandwich

realistic enough to swing the fleet behind the restoration of the king in 1660. For this he was created Baron Montagu, Viscount Hinchinbroke and Earl of Sandwich and reappointed Vice Admiral to the king's brother, James. He then reorganised the fleet, with the able assistance of Samuel Pepys, Secretary to the Navy.

His younger son married the heiress of Sir Francis Wortley, and their son adopted the name Wortley-Montagu. He married Lady Mary Pierrepont, better known as Lady Mary Wortley-Montagu, the pioneer of smallpox inoculation. Another grandson, also Edward, married the well-known blue stocking, or learned lady, Elizabeth Robinson (Mrs Montagu). Neither husband showed any distinction whatsoever.

There were many younger branches of the family, mainly in Lackham, Devon and Norfolk, while the family seat continued to be at Kimbolton Castle, and Brampton, Northamptonshire.

One Montagu family definitely not related to the Montacutes is that of Lord Swaythling, who was descended from Louis Samuel, merchant. His son, anglicised as Montagu, adopted that as an additional surname to Samuel in 1894, when he was created a baronet, and the barony followed in 1907. Edwin Samuel Montagu was an MP like his father, a junior minister from 1910 and Minister for Munitions in 1916, then Secretary of State for India till 1922.

Should I really be the Earl of Mucke?

Every peerage family has a fairly detailed entry in *Burke's Peerage* – *Debrett* is much more limited, to recent generations only. If you have been told you are related, and share the family surname (see the list on pages 96 – 114), then have a very good look at the printed pedigree. In most cases, this is complete for the last several generations, from the 9th to the 14th Earl for example, but, if there are plenty of males born, it seems that the main line will never run out, so the compiler may have omitted all the children of the sons six or seven generations back. What he will write, if there *were* children, is 'and had issue'. This could be worth following up, to see what happened to those children of the younger son of the 6th Earl. Sometimes even in the main line, half a dozen children are named and it says 'with other issue'. This is not so promising, since they are usually children who died young, or daughters (who were not taken very seriously in families with plenty of sons).

ARE WE RELATED?

Be wary of the family tradition that of course your own ancestor was the eldest son, but his father didn't like him, and cut him out of the inheritance. This simply can't be done. If a man is the eldest son of a duke or earl, in the fullness of time, if he survives, he will become duke or earl.

HAMPDEN HOBART

Even a more distant male heir will inherit. The days when working for a living disqualified a genuine heir (like Percy the Trunkmaker) have gone. The fabled John Hampden, 'the Patriot', who started a civil war caused partly by his unwillingness to pay his taxes (which he thought unlawful), left no male heirs after four generations, so the succession to his estates went to the heirs of his daughters, first of Ruth Trevor, then in 1824 to the Hobarts, who became Hampden Hobart and then Earls of Buckinghamshire. When Sir John Hampden-Hobart-(Mercer-Henderson), Earl of Buckinghamshire died, his heir was his second cousin, who was found working as plain Cecil Hobart, a gardener for Southend-on-Sea town council. And Vere Frederick Cecil Hobart-Hampden duly became Earl for a few years, died childless and was succeeded by his third cousin of the half-blood.

HASTINGS

In the past, this type of inheritance was more difficult. The 10th Earl of Huntingdon died in 1789, childless, and his only surviving sister, the Countess of Moira, inherited his four baronies of Hastings, Botreaux, de Moleyns and Hungerford, but the earldom was not heritable by females. Lord Moira angled for the greater title, but there was a very distant male heir.

The 9th Earl had realised his son would never marry, and had sought out the next heir. Through lack of males for many generations, this was a *very* distant cousin, Henry Hastings, descended from a younger son of the 2nd Earl. Henry had two surviving sons, Theophilus and George, who were taken under the wing of the 9th Earl. Theophilus became a clergyman, and young George was betrothed to the elder daughter of the Earl, sister to Lady Moira, but she died just before the wedding.

When the 10th Earl died, Rev. Theophilus Hastings actually called himself Earl – which he was by right – but made no headway in getting any estates from Lord Moira, who pretended to be uncertain if there were nearer heirs. George went into the army, and was rash enough to entrust two of his sons to Moira to bring up. He put them in the navy, sent them to the disease-ridden West Indies, and they duly died off.

The remaining son, Hans Francis Hastings, jibbed at going to the Indies as well, and made his own modest way in the army, sure he was heir to the earldom, but in no position to challenge the powerful Moira. Then an Irish lawyer took up his cause, proving that every possible intervening male in the family had died off. Lord Moira is supposed to have ripped pages out of church registers to frustrate him, not realising there were alternative copies. Eventually, the lawyer got all the evidence, presented it on Hans' behalf to the House of Lords, and Hans got his earldom in 1819, 30 years after the death of the last Earl.

The four baronies went to the eldest son of Lady Moira on her death in 1808, and he was made up to Marquess of Hastings (a step up from an earldom), married the Countess of Loudon in her own right, and was given a couple of other titles for good measure. So Hans Francis won, in 1819, but was outranked by his rival. However, revenge came in 1868, when the Marquess's grandsons died unmarried and the title lapsed, while the earldom continued. The eldest granddaughter of the Marquess became Countess of Loudon, the second took her mother's title of Baroness Grey of Ruthyn, and the other baronies were split between them, which left the youngest sisters and co-heirs out in the cold. (The Countess of Romney presumably was happy with what she had, but plain Mrs Kirwan of Moyne may have regretted agreeing to this when things got difficult for Anglo-Irish landowners.)

When daughters will not do

Often the senior line of the family starts running out of male heirs, mostly because they tend to marry heiresses, and you don't get to be an heiress if you have any brothers. The risk in marrying a girl from a family short of male heirs is that she will produce only daughters herself.

There is nothing wrong with daughters, and in a perfect world, they would simply inherit title and estates, but this is not the way it works in the strange world of hereditary peerages. The implication is that the head of the family will go off to war and fight in single combat, in heavy plate armour, to preserve the estates, so, in normal thinking, he needs to be a big, tough man. Most of our dukes and marquesses do not do a great deal of work with sword and battle-axe these days, but the rules of inheritance ensure that only a male can inherit most English or UK titles. A number of Scottish titles and ancient baronies are heritable by females, though the idea is that the husband will take over the name and the mortal combat.

TEMPLE-GRENVILLE

Inevitably, some families do run out of male heirs altogether, and then the title becomes extinct. The Temple family of Stowe had stacked up an impressive range of titles by the 19th century. Starting as baronets (Temple), successive generations angled for and got higher titles – Baron Temple, Viscount Cobham, Earl Temple – and even when the male Temple line failed, the last one had the wit to ensure that the estates would pass to his sister Hester, Mrs Grenville, and that her son would get the title of Lord Grenville and Earl Temple. Successive Grenvilles advanced to Marquess of Buckingham, then Duke of Buckingham, married the heiress of the Duke of Chandos and acquired that title too, with the Scottish barony of Kinloss as an optional extra. But then the whole scheme came apart, for the last duke had daughters only.

There had been some planning for contingencies, and when he died, the two dukedoms became extinct, but the title of Earl Temple went to his sister's eldest son, William Stephen Gore-Langton. The title of Lord Cobham went back to the male heirs of a sister of Hester Grenville, the barons Lyttleton.

Mary, the last Duke's eldest daughter, got just the barony of Kinloss, and her sister Mrs Hadaway got nothing. Possibly the Duke had hoped his girls would marry some other grandee, a duke, who could suitably add the titles to his. But first the younger girl married an artillery colonel in 1882, then Mary, his pride, insisted on marrying the boy next door, Major Luis Courthope Morgan, in 1884. The Duke, happily a widower since 1874, suddenly cast round for a new bride, and married young Alice Montgomery in 1885, hoping for a son to inherit. Sadly, Alice could not oblige (nor for a second husband later).

The Duke went frustrated to the grave in 1889, leaving Lady Mary Morgan, Baroness Kinloss, an estate much decreased by the wild extravagance of the last three dukes. She let the mansion and lived more modestly on her husband's estate, taking the name Morgan-Grenville for her family. Their adored eldest son was killed in World War One, and the heir was now the second son, a clergyman, Luis Morgan-Grenville, with very democratic ideas. He married the local blacksmith's daughter (a rather accomplished young lady nevertheless) and when the aged Lady Kinloss died, just after Luis, his eldest daughter inherited the barony.

CHAPTER 5

DUCAL FAMILIES

CAVENDISH

Although the main title of the Cavendish family is that of Duke of Devonshire, there is no noticeable connection with that county at all – it was just the title going spare at the time when the family were due to be 'made up'.

The first Cavendish who can be proved to have existed is Sir John. He must have come from a reasonable, free, landowning family, since he became a lawyer, ending as Chief Justice of the Court of King's Bench in 1366. He cleverly married Alice de Odynseles, heiress of the small manor of Cavendish Overhall in Suffolk (and it may be he took his name from this). A younger son, John, as Esquire to the Body of Richard II, claimed to have finished off Wat Tyler, the leader of the Peasants' Revolt, after the Mayor of London attacked him and was resisted. He got a knighthood for it, anyway.

George Cavendish, in Henry VIII's time, shines out as an honest man who was not afraid of standing up for his principles. He was a clerk to Cardinal Wolsey, and when that prelate was being victimised by royal sycophants, stood by him to the end. Unusually – for Henry was not big on appreciation of those who resisted him – the king was so impressed that he kept him on in royal service.

It was George's younger brother William who made the fortunate marriage on which his family's wealth is based. Elizabeth, heiress of Sir John Hardwick of Hardwick Hall in Derbyshire, known as 'Bess of Hardwick', first married Robert Barley, who did not last. She then cast about for a more suitable mate, and found Sir William Cavendish. Veteran of two marriages already, he was one of the commissioners for the Dissolution of the Monasteries, became Treasurer of the

King's Chamber under Henry VIII and remained so through the next two short reigns. So he was rich and tactful, given the violent religious changes of those times.

Bess and William raised numerous children, of whom six survived to adulthood, and Bess also kept herself amused by building mansions: Hardwick was refurbished out of recognition, and she build Oldcotes Hall and the magnificent Chatsworth. William died in 1556, but even though Bess was married twice more, to William St Loe and then to the Earl of Shrewsbury, she never forgot him. Her Cavendish children were advanced whenever the opportunity offered.

Her eldest son married Shrewsbury's daughter, but both died young. Her third son was found the heiress Baroness Ogle, and their son became Duke of Newcastle, though, with male heirs failing, the title passed to the husband of a granddaughter, John Holles. Daughter Frances married Sir Henry Pierrepont, and their descendants were Earls and Dukes of Kingston. Daughter Elizabeth married Charles Stuart, Earl of Lennox, closely allied to the Scottish royal family, and their daughter, Arabella Stuart, was put forward as a possible queen, instead of her unattractive cousin, James VI of Scotland. This nearly cost the by then ancient Bess her head, but Arabella died childless in 1607, which was considered an acceptable alternative. Mary married the 7th Earl of Shrewsbury, and from them are descended the Dukes of Norfolk.

8th Duke of Devonshire, Marquis of Hartington

But the prize went to the second son, Sir William, heir after his brother died. He was created Earl of Devon (until someone pointed out there was one already, so the title was changed to

ARE WE RELATED?

Devonshire). The family in 1694 were promoted to Dukes of Devonshire, with Marquess of Hartington as subsidiary title. A couple of generations later, they picked up the barony of Clifford and were created Earls of Burlington (the title of Lady Clifford's father). This barony went into abeyance between sisters when a duke died childless, but there were always ample male heirs to carry on the line.

When a member of the family married the heiress of the Earl of Northampton, he didn't get the title, but her surname, Compton, was used for many of their descendants. One of the younger sons, Charles Compton Cavendish, was created Baron Chesham.

Since then, luxuriating in the possession of the three most magnificent mansions in the kingdom, the Cavendish family have taken a prominent part in the life of the country, even breaking into politics in Victorian times. Lord Frederick Cavendish, a younger son, hit the headlines in 1882 when, as the newly arrived Secretary for Ireland, he was murdered in Phoenix Park by the terrorists of the day, sparking off angry reprisals.

His uncle, Spencer Compton Cavendish, long Marquess of Hartington, was known as Harty-Tarty, and occupied a number of government posts, including Secretary for War, Secretary for Ireland, Secretary for India and Postmaster General. To everyone's surprise (including his own) he got married for the first time at the age of 59, to the sexy Countess Luise Von Alten, widow of the Duke of Manchester. He rapidly withdrew into politics again, as Lord President of the Council, and his wife swanned round the salons of London as 'the Double Duchess'.

Since then things have quietened down, but the 11th Duke was on the fringe of turbulence when he married one of the 'Mitford girls', who included the authoress Nancy and the Hitler groupie, Unity. Duchess Deborah is the youngest, prettiest and most sensible one.

Related in name and maternally in blood are the **Cavendish-Bentincks**, Dukes of Portland. The Bentincks were part of the ancient nobility of the Duchy of Guelders, who came over with William III for the pickings which his new kingdom might provide for loyal servants. Hans Willem Bentinck was appointed Groom of the Stole and first Gentleman of the Bedchamber, and created Baron Cirencester, Viscount Woodstock and Earl of Portland. His son was created Duke of Portland and Marquess of Titchfield.

The Cavendish link came through Margaret Cavendish, daughter and co-heir of Henry, Duke of Newcastle, who married John Holles, Earl of Clare, who was given the title of Duke of Newcastle. The Holles family also ran out to daughters, one of whom married a Pelham, newly created Duke of Newcastle; another heiress married into the Harley family, Earls of Oxford, and her daughter was Lady Margaret Cavendish Harley, known to the poets as 'my pretty, noble, Peggy'. Their son reinforced the connection by marrying Dorothy, daughter of the 4th Duke of Devonshire, and adopted by royal licence the name of Cavendish-Bentinck for his family for ever.

The Dukes of Portland were great connoisseurs of art, and collected many pieces from Greece. The Portland Vase has been placed in the British Museum for all to admire. Even before this, the family followed the gentry tradition of allowing respectable people to visit their mansion, in their absence, and view the treasures (under escort of the housekeeper).

The 4th Duke had four sons, but all of them died as bachelors, throwing the inheritance open to the next heir.

The 3rd Duke had had three sons, of whom the second died childless. The third son had married Anne Wellesley, illegitimate daughter of Wellington's brother, Marquess Wellesley, and herself the divorced wife of Sir William Abdy (which must have caused a bit of a stir). Their eldest son, Rev. Charles Frederick Cavendish, caused even more talk when he married at 21 a beautiful gipsy girl, Sinetta Lambourne, whose father was a horse dealer in Oxfordshire. All her children died young, and so did she. He then married more soberly, Caroline Burnaby, daughter of a Leicester gentleman, and had three more daughters, Nina and the twins Violet and Hyacinthe. The youngest girl married a Mr Jessup and had descendants in Philadelphia.

If Nina had been a boy, she would have become Duke of Portland. As it was, she married Claude, 14th Earl of Strathmore, in 1881, and had ten children, of whom the youngest daughter was Elizabeth, the Queen Mother.

The dukedom went to Nina's first cousin, William John Arthur Cavendish-Bentinck (6th Duke) and continues with his grandson. The only scandal in the family after this may have been the mild shock at the outrageous behaviour of the 5th Duke's sister, Lady Ottoline Morrell, a society hostess who collected rather raffish literary men and artists in the decadent 1920s.

ARE WE RELATED?

HOWARD

The Dukes of Norfolk are the premier peers of England, standing next to the royal family, and hereditary Earls Marshal. As such, they are responsible for organising coronations, which don't come often, and state funerals, which involves the participation of a rigidly Catholic family in Protestant rituals.

A *ho-ward*, or *hay-ward*, by definition, is the manorial official who looks after the hedges and fences of the estate, keeping out wolves and people from the next manor. From these small beginnings, the family became very minor land-owners in Wiggenhall, Norfolk, and a bright son went into the law. Knighted, one married a bastard daughter of a minor royal; their son displayed a flair for organising naval protection for the Norfolk coast and cleverly married the heiress of Sir John Boys. From then on, they sought out heiresses of increasing importance, until a younger son, Sir Robert Howard, picked the plum. Margaret Mowbray was elder daughter of Thomas, Duke of Norfolk, by his wife, the heiress of Fitzalan, Earl of Arundel. Her grandmother was Lady Segrave in her own right, and daughter of Margaret Plantagenet, heiress of the royal Thomas de Brotherton, Duke of Norfolk. With that impeccable pedigree, and a lot of wealth from the earlier marriages, plus his talents as naval and military commander, their son, John, was naturally created Duke of Norfolk and his heir, Earl of Surrey. A loyal man in difficult times, he refused to betray his king, Richard III, at Bosworth though he was warned:

Jockey of Norfolk, be not so bold, for Dickon thy master is bought and sold

He was killed in battle and attainted, but his son was restored four years later. His daughter Elizabeth married Thomas, Lord Rochford and was the mother of Anne Boleyn, second queen of Henry VIII, who was executed on trumped up charges. As if losing one granddaughter to the axe was not enough, a second was offered up: Catherine Howard, who also married Henry and was beheaded, probably for genuine guilt. Another son of the restored Duke turned his attention to Scotland and made a bid for the hand of Lady Margaret Douglas, daughter of Henry VIII's sister, Dowager Queen of Scotland, by her second husband. This didn't go down too well and he was imprisoned in the Tower, where he died.

The 3rd Duke married Princess Anne, a daughter of Edward IV, but she died while still young. He was implicated in the rising of 1546, and attainted, while his son, Henry, Earl of Surrey, brilliant soldier and talented poet, was beheaded.

The 3rd Duke of Norfolk   *The 17th Duke of Norfolk*

The Duke, as a good Catholic, was restored to his honours in 1553 by Mary I. His grandson, Thomas, the 4th Duke, did not learn by experience and intrigued with Mary, Queen of Scots in 1572 and was beheaded. The less than sensible antics of the previous decades were redeemed by the glorious exploits of Lord Howard of Effingham, who was instrumental in defeating the Spanish Armada in 1588. Philip Howard, eldest son of the 5th Duke, had to make do with his mother's inheritance, the earldom of Arundel. He and two of his brothers married the three heiresses of the barony of Dacre, and the two younger ones were given titles, eventually, as Earl of Suffolk and Lord Howard de Walden, and Earl of Carlisle. The male Suffolk line failed and the minor title passed through the Griffins to the Herveys to the Scott-Ellises.

The minor titles were restored in 1604, and the dukedom of Norfolk in 1660, as part of Charles II's reconciliation scheme. Charles, in so far as he was interested in religion at all, was vaguely Catholic, and his brother James definitely so, and a Cardinal Howard of the family was almoner to Charles's wife, Catherine of Braganza.

ARE WE RELATED?

The 7th Duke arranged James's coronation and his younger son, in right of his manor of Worksop, 'provided the king with a right hand glove and supported his arm while holding the sceptre' at the ceremony.

With the death of the 9th Duke, who left only nieces as close kin, the family baronies went into abeyance and then were divided between their descendants, but the dukedom reverted back to a distant cousin, Charles, as 10th Duke. The 15th Duke rashly married not one, but two heiresses of ancient titles, and although he had a son from each marriage, one died young, the other produced daughters only. When the 16th Duke died, his eldest daughter inherited her grandmother's barony of Herries, but the dukedom again reverted, going back to the line of the younger son of the 13th Duke, created Lord Howard of Glossop. Even this line was producing only one son per generation, but when the later Lord Howard of Glossop took a gamble and married an heiress, Mona, Baroness Beaumont, she overturned expectations by producing four sons and four daughters, all of whose names began with an M. The new Duke, Miles, produced two sons, so the succession is safe. His daughter Lady Carina married David Frost, the television presenter.

HAMILTON

This Scottish family was originally descended from one of the Normans who poured over the border in search of land freed from the fairly tight control of the English kings. The progenitor is supposed to be Robert de Bellomonte, Earl of Leicester. The first known Hamilton turned up in Alexander II's time, when Gilbert Hamilton of Cadzow married the daughter of the Earl of Moray. Early, younger sons spun off to acquire their own lands, in Innerwick (Earls of Haddington), Preston, Cambuskeith, Orbieston and Silverton.

James of Cadzow, 1st Lord Hamilton, married a daughter of the Earl of Strathearn, and then Princess Mary, eldest daughter of James II and widow of the Earl of Arran. Their daughter married the king's cousin, the Earl of Lennox, and the son somehow acquired his mother's first husband's title of Earl of Arran. When James IV died, leaving a baby daughter as queen, her cousin, the 2nd Earl of Arran, was appointed regent and recognised as the next heir, a heady combination, but to his credit the child survived to become Mary, Queen of Scots. He accepted a bribe of a French dukedom (of Chatellerault) to fix the marriage of the little queen to the Dauphin of France and himself married Margaret Douglas, daughter of James Earl of Morton, also a regent.

One son became a marquess and the grandson Duke of Hamilton, but the line ran out of males, and the heiress, Anne, Duchess of Hamilton, carried the title into the Douglas family.

However, the youngest son, Claude Hamilton, became Lord Paisley and his loyalty to James VI and I got him advanced to Earl of Abercorn. The elder son and his son inherited, but for lack of males the title reverted to the younger son, Claude, who went to Ireland and became Lord Strabane. His sons in turn, and a grandson of another, became earls. They were advanced to marquess in 1790, and in 1868 to Duke of Abercorn, also going to some trouble in 1862 to reclaim the French dukedom of Chatellerault, a title no one had used since the first bearer. The family has been involved in politics in a small way as MPs, two briefly as junior ministers, and several served in the army or militia, but the really interesting character was Jocelyn Patrick Hamilton, who took his MA at Oxford, was briefly a barrister, went to Canada, studied surgery and osteopathy and also lectured in history at Toronto University, before settling in Ireland.

The 3rd Duke's daughter, Lady Cynthia, married in 1919 the then Earl Spencer, and was grandmother of Diana Spencer and the present Earl.

DOUGLAS-HAMILTON

Paradoxically, the Duke of Hamilton and Brandon is paternally a Douglas, stemming from the Earl of Angus, illegitimate son of the Earl of Douglas and the Countess of Mar – they were a wild lot then. They were always in the thick of any rebellion, and only the fact that two branches, the Red Douglas and the Black Douglas, rarely took the same side saved the family from extinction. The Angus Douglases were the more circumspect and steadily advanced. Archibald, 4th Earl, married Margaret Tudor, the widow of James II of Scotland, and their small daughter Margaret was a honeypot for all adventurers. They married her to the Earl of Lennox, close kin to the king, and her son, Henry, Lord Darnley, married his cousin, Mary, Queen of Scots. However, he treated her badly and was noisily eliminated by an explosion, by one of her more competent suitors. Their son, James VI, was always frightened of assassination thereafter, but he did inherit his great-grandmother's claim to the English throne, becoming James I in 1603.

Failure of male heirs sent the earldom into junior lines twice, but the family steadily picked up more titles – Earl of Forfar, Marquess of Douglas, Earl of

Selkirk, Earl of Dumbarton, etc. Finally, little Archibald Douglas, succeeding as 3rd Marquess at six, was advanced at nine to a dukedom, with other subsidiary titles. It was too much – he sat back under shock till he was 64 before marrying in 1758, and it was too late, for he died childless three years later.

Then came the uproar, for his only sister, Lady Jane, had run off years before with Sir John Stewart of Grandtully, which caused her brother to wash his hands of her. She was then either 44 or 50, old enough to make up her own mind. She died in 1753. But now young Archibald James Edward Stewart came forward, claiming he was the survivor of twin children of hers. Opinion was much divided, for the age of the lady seemed to cast doubts on this. The 'Douglas cause' ran and ran, until in 1769 Archie, who had adopted the name Douglas, was adjudged to be Jane's son, and made Earl of Douglas.

The male heir of line claimed through William, Lord Selkirk, who had married Anne, Duchess of Hamilton. The family were henceforth known as Douglas-Hamilton.

LEVESON-GOWER

The origins of the Scottish family who were Earls and Dukes of Sutherland are, for once, not Norman but Flemish. Freskin settled in Moray by 1160, and his descendant, William, was ennobled by Alexander II as Earl of Sutherland, which is at the northern tip of Scotland. The 5th Earl married a daughter of Robert Bruce, and her brother, King David I, raised the earldom into a regality, so the family were truly 'kings of the north'. Two Sutherland earls went quietly mad, so the estates devolved on Elizabeth, Countess of Sutherland, and her husband, Adam Gordon. The 11th Earl died by poison in 1567. He and his wife and son were visiting Helmisdale, castle of the widowed Isobel Gordon, his aunt, whose small son was the next heir. She, intent on securing his inheritance, poisoned their food, but the Earl, suspecting something was wrong, warned his son, who arrived late, not to eat any. The Earl and Countess died a few days later but the heir was saved.

The earldom continued in the Gordon family until 1766, when the 18th Earl, the last male, died aged 31, leaving a baby daughter only. There were a number of junior branches of the Gordon family, but a descendant of the old Sutherlands also claimed the title – saying that the Countess Elizabeth should never have inherited and conveyed it to her husband in 1500 (slow thinkers, these

Sutherlands). The court decided that her inheritance was valid, which meant that so now was the claim of the only daughter of the 18th Earl, Elizabeth, now aged five.

In 1785 she married, not a good Scot, but an Englishman, George Granville Leveson Gower (pronounced *Looson Gore*) then Viscount Trentham and Earl Gower and later Marquess of Stafford. He was created Duke of Sutherland, while his wife continued to be Countess in her own right, which is confusing.

The new Duke thought that thousands of marginally productive acres of land in the north of Scotland were not much use except as grouse moor or fishing rivers, and ordered his agents to clear out all the crofters who were scratching a living, as their ancestors had done for generations. The Highland Clearances caused great distress and bitterness which make the Sutherland name a dirty word to this day. The Duke, being a mere Englishman, probably knew no better, but the old Countess was a Scot and should somehow have defended her inheritance better. Most of the harm was done after her death. The later generations of the family spent most of their time in England, where successive duchesses were Mistresses of the Robes to the Queen.

The male heirs of the 4th Duke ran out again (as a punishment, some held) and the niece of the 5th Duke inherited as Countess of Sutherland and Lady Strathnaver, while the next male, descended from the second son of the 1st Duke and the Countess, inherited that title. This was the family of Francis, Earl of Ellesmere, who took the surname Egerton in preference to Leveson-Gower.

There are no other males of the Leveson-Gower family descended from the Countess of Sutherland, but a number from earlier generations, many with the middle name Gresham, after a marriage between William Leveson-Gower and the heiress of Sir John Gresham in 1804. It is not a name which is popular in Scotland, or in certain parts of Canada where the expelled crofters went. There are many Gordons, though only those of Gordonstoun are kin to the Sutherland earls. There are also likely to be actual Sutherlands, descended from the Sutherlands of Forsie, who tried to claim the earldom in 1766. Their Scottish home is Dunrobin Castle, and the smaller house at the Tongue of Lairg, but Sutton Place, in Surrey, was their more recent home, until it was acquired by Paul Getty.

ARE WE RELATED?

SEYMOUR

The St Maur family were settled in estates in Monmouthshire by Edward I's time, and founded their fortunes when a St Maur married Cecily Beauchamp, who, by intervening deaths, became in her descendants heiress of the 3rd Lord Beauchamp of Somerset. Later heiresses were less prestigious, but a great deal of money came with the daughter of a Bristol city knight. They might have remained quiet country squires in Wiltshire, but there was a pretty daughter, Jane, who caught the eye of Henry VIII, and gave him the longed for son he needed. She died soon after his birth, but the delighted king rewarded her kinsfolk by making her eldest brother Viscount Beauchamp, then Earl of Hertford. Henry left him as executor and governor to his young nephew, and this was rapidly taken advantage of, so that the governor of the boy became Protector of the Kingdom. He was created Baron Seymour and Duke of Somerset, Earl Marshal and organiser of the coronation. He also took charge of the army and invaded Scotland, defeated the French and saw off the Emperor – he had merely been waiting for a chance to rule. His younger brother was created Lord Seymour of Sudeley and Lord High Admiral and in a few days married the widowed Queen, Catherine Parr. She had custody of the young Princess Elizabeth, and Thomas Seymour was soon making advances to her instead; he was convicted of high treason and beheaded in 1549.

The mighty Duke of Northumberland, jealous of the Seymours, intrigued until the boy Edward ungratefully signed his uncle Somerset's death warrant in 1552. His diary observed coldly: 'Today my Lord of Somerset was beheaded; rather chilly morning, but no rain' (or words to that effect).

Somerset had married a minor heiress, Catherine Filliol, and had a surviving son by her, Sir Edward Seymour of Berry Pomeroy. However, his second wife was heiress to the barony of Fitzwarine and potentially the earldom of Bath, so his major honours were reserved for her children. His daughter, strangely, had been allowed to marry the son of his great rival, John Dudley, Duke of Northumberland, but they had no children and he was beheaded for treason in his turn, for supporting the claim of Lady Jane Grey against Queen Mary. The only heir of the second family was Edward Seymour, who got no titles on his father's death, since he was attainted, but was given a new earldom of Hertford by Elizabeth when she succeeded in 1558.

Instead of being grateful, Edward promptly married Lady Catherine Grey, sister of the beheaded Lady Jane Grey, who had a claim to the throne through her grandmother, Princess Mary Tudor, Duchess of Suffolk. When she was seen to be pregnant (for the second time) they were both thrown into the Tower, where somehow they managed to have another child, who died young, with his mother. The Earl of Hertford was fined £15,000 for violating a maid of the blood royal. He married twice more but without issue. The eldest son, Edward, Lord Beauchamp died before his father, but his son succeeded eventually to his grandfather's earldom.

Not learning by experience, William Seymour as a young man of 22 had paid court to 35-year-old Arabella Stuart, heiress of the Earl of Lennox, cousin and rival of James I. He married her secretly in 1610, but fled abroad on discovery of the marriage and Arabella was put into the Tower alone, where she died aged 40 in 1615. Allowed to return, in 1616 he married Frances, daughter of Robert Devereux, Earl of Essex, Elizabeth's sometime favourite, had eight children and was gradually restored to his titles; he was even appointed governor to the small Prince Charles. His gallantry in the Civil War earned him the title Marquess of Hertford and even his great-grandfather's dukedom of Somerset, just before his death in 1660. A son and grandson followed but the male line from William then ended, and the title reverted to his brother's sons.

The young 5th Duke went on the Grand Tour of Europe in 1678, and chatted up some Italian girls outside an inn; unfortunately their brother took exception and shot him. This left only the 6th Duke, his brother, who married the Lady Elizabeth Percy, heiress of the Earl of Northumberland. Their son, Algernon, became 7th Duke of Somerset as well as Baron Percy and Earl of Northumberland, with a clutch of other titles from the Seymour side.

But Algernon's only son died at 19, so he had to make provision for what happened on his death, which occurred in 1750. His only daughter, who married Sir Hugh Smithson, got the Northumberland title, which was made up to a dukedom. His nephews, sons of his only surviving sister, Lady Wyndham, became Earl of Egremont and Earl of Thomond. The Seymour titles at last reverted to the first family of the original Duke of Somerset, the Seymours of Berry Pomeroy – very handily, for they had had their castle destroyed in the Civil War and were only with difficulty rebuilding their estates, by selected marriages to heiresses.

ARE WE RELATED?

The 6th Baronet claimed the dukedom in 1750, greased the right palms and had his claim agreed. His half-brother, already Lord Conway in right of his mother, and a court official, became Lord Beauchamp, Earl, and then Marquess of Hertford and Earl of Yarmouth. A descendant married Prince Victor of Hohenlohe-Langenburg, son of Queen Victoria's beloved half-sister, Fedore, and was mother of 'Count Edward Gleichen', who served loyally and brilliantly in several wars.

There was only one major blip in the smooth succession of Dukes of Somerset, when Algernon Seymour, 15th Duke, died in 1923 with absolutely no close male relatives left. It was necessary to go back to the fourth son of the 8th Duke, the Rev. Francis Seymour, Dean of Wells, who had left one son only; but that son had three sons, all with sons of their own. His eldest son's grandson, Edward Hamilton Seymour, son of another Rev. Francis, now claimed the dukedom. The House of Lords granted his claim in 1925, so he became 16th Duke, and was succeeded in 1931 by his only son, Evelyn. The 17th Duke had three sons, but only one survived, and one grandson, showing how fragile can be the line even for a gentry family in modern times.

GORDON-LENNOX

Although the cousins of the royal Stuart line held the title of Earl of Lennox, the male heirs failed, and the surname Lennox was revived for one of Charles II's bastard sons, Charles, born 1672, by Louise de Kerouaille, created Duchess of Portsmouth for services rendered. She was devoutly Catholic and not a popular person, and when the mob attacked what they thought was her carriage, out popped the head of Nell Gwyn, who grinned and assured them: 'No, no, friends, I am the *Protestant* whore.'

Charles was created (English titles) Duke of Richmond in 1675, with lesser titles of Earl of March and Baron of Settrington, and was then given the Scottish titles of Duke of Lennox, Earl of Darnley and Lord Torbolton. His son inherited the Duchy of Aubigny in France through his grandmother in 1734, and married a co-heiress of Lord Cadogan. One of his daughters married the architect Henry Fox, Lord Holland, and was a celebrated political hostess and intriguer. Another, Lady Sarah, might have become queen, for George III as a prince fancied her – but she was turned down by the court, in favour of a German princess, Caroline of Ansbach. The voluptuous Sarah was a (rather indignant) bridesmaid to the skinny Caroline.

The 4th Duke (called Charles like all his predecessors and successors) married Charlotte Gordon, eventual heiress of the family, and their grandson in 1876 received a new creation of the dukedom of Gordon. His successors had the rare distinction of being triple dukes. This 6th Duke did make a brief incursion into politics, serving as President of the Poor Law Board and then of the Board of Trade, in neither of which fields he had first-hand experience. His son had married the granddaughter of the economist David Ricardo, who may have been able to provide tips.

The 8th Duke's half-sister, Lady Helen Gordon-Lennox, over 50 when World War Two started, abandoned her post as Mistress of the Robes to the Queen, and joined the transport branch of the Nursing Yeomanry, taking over the running of the unit funded by the Duchess of Northumberland, from 1941 to 1946.

The connection with Scotland (despite the hereditary office of Constable of Inverness) is remote, and the family home is handily placed near a racecourse in Surrey. The 9th Duke married a vicar's daughter from Buckinghamshire, to the chagrin of the aristocratic mammas with marriageable daughters.

The coat of arms quarters the royal arms within a bordure (to show illegitimate descent) with those of Gordon.

BEAUCLERK

Charles II's sons by Nell Gwyn were given the royal names of Charles and James, and – for want of any other surname – Beauclerk, 'good writer', which was probably a warped comment on their mother's lack of education. The title of Duke of St Albans was bestowed in 1681, when Charles was eleven, after some strong complaints from his mother that all the other bastards had titles. He was created Registrar of the Court of Chancery (which was run by officials) and, rather more suitably, Royal Falconer. In 1694 he was married to Lady Diana de Vere, heiress of the ancient earldom of Oxford, but he was not given the title, though the surname Vere was incorporated before Beauclerk, and a third son was given the title of Baron de Vere. When Lord Vere's son inherited the dukedom, the two titles came together.

The 8th Duke at 27 married the mature, and very rich, widow of Thomas Coutts, the banker, née Harriet Mellon, a former actress, who enjoyed being a duchess for ten years, even if it cost her some of her inherited wealth. Unusually for those days, she retained control over her money, and left it in 1837 not

Nell Gwyn

meekly to her husband, but to old Thomas's granddaughter, 'the faymale heiress, Miss Angaly Coutts', daughter of Sir Francis Burdett and Sophia (née Coutts). Angela was a strong-minded, independent philanthropist, who caused great shock when at almost 67 she suddenly married a toy-boy, William Ashmead Bartlett. No one had raised a fuss at the similar marriage of the Duke to Harriet Coutts, or of ageing Thomas Coutts to the young actress. Angela (Baroness Burdett-Coutts) lived to be 92.

The Dukes of St Albans lived for most of the 19th century in Ireland. The senior line ran out of males, and a cousin inherited, who had served with distinction in military intelligence in World War Two; he moved to Monte Carlo after the war.

FITZROY

Charles II's younger son, Henry, by Barbara Palmer, Duchess of Cleveland, was born in 1663, named Fitz-Roy (son of the king) and created in 1672 Baron Sudbury, Viscount Ipswich and Earl of Euston; in 1675, the additional title of Duke of Grafton was bestowed. Aged nine, and more formally at the age of 16, he was married to the heiress of the Earl of Arlington. Given continuing favour by his uncle, James II, he was one of the first to desert him for William III when the latter invaded. He fought for 'King Billy' at the Siege of Cork.

Their only child, Charles, inherited the dukedom when he was seven, in 1690, and the earldom of Arlington when his mother died in 1722. Three of his sons died before him, and his heir was his grandson, Augustus Henry, the 3rd Duke. He became a politician and served a term as Prime Minister in 1766. He married Anne Liddell, heiress of Lord Ravensworth, whom he divorced in 1769 after she abandoned her three children and ran off with a handsome Irish earl. The Duke married the lady he had waiting in the wings, by whom he had another six children – this family has never had a problem producing reserve stocks of males for when the eldest son dies childless.

The 4th Duke married Charlotte Waldegrave, whose pretty mother was Maria, the illegitimate granddaughter of Sir Robert Walpole, the famous Prime Minister. She first married Earl Waldegrave, then the royal Duke of Gloucester (brother of George III), known as Silly Billy even to his friends.

ARE WE RELATED?

The distinguished member of this family was a cousin, Admiral Fitzroy, who invented a barometer for the use of the navy. The Fitzroy barometer is still a type found in many old houses and very collectable.

A younger brother of the 3rd Duke was created Baron Southampton; his descendants were mainly military men, with the occasional naval officer thrown in. From time to time they married their Grafton cousins. The younger son of the 3rd Baron, after a distinguished military career, entered politics and was elected Speaker of the House of Commons in 1928. He died in office in 1943, and his widow was given the title which retiring Speakers are offered, becoming Viscountess Daventry, a title their son inherited in 1962.

The family seat of the Dukes of Grafton is Euston Hall, near Thetford, Norfolk.

OSBORNE

The dukedom of Leeds is one of the titles which has comparatively recently become extinct. The originators of the family were not military knights or country squires, but good solid merchants. Edward Osborne, as an apprentice, courted his master's daughter, Dick Whittington style, and married Anne Hewett, the daughter of a former Lord Mayor; in 1583, he was himself chosen Mayor and knighted. He had several children by her, including Sir Hewett Osborne. He acquired a small property in Kiveton, Yorkshire (which may possibly have been where the family originated).

His grandson, Edward Osborne, a Royalist Member of Parliament (and so in a small minority) bought a baronetcy and also rose by marriage, first to a daughter of Viscount Fauconberg, then to Anne Walmesely, whose mother was the Earl of Danby's sister and grandmother, a co-heiress of Lord Latymer.

Their son, Sir Thomas Osborne, married in 1651 Bridget, daughter of the Earl of Lindsay, Lord Great Chamberlain, and became Lord High Treasurer to the impecunious Charles II, for whom he raised money, and President of the Council under William III. Charles made him Viscount Osborne and Viscount Latymer and then Earl of Danby, in 1674. William topped this by creating him Marquess of Carmarthen in 1689 and Duke of Leeds in 1694.

One of his daughters married Charles FitzCharles, Earl of Plymouth, a son of the king by Catherine Pegge, but there were no heirs. His heir, the 2nd Duke, picked up another title as Lord Dunblane in Scotland, and was Baron Osborne of Kiveton, Yorkshire. Thomas, the 4th Duke of Leeds, married the heiress of Francis, Earl of Godolphin, granddaughter of the great Duke of Marlborough, and the name Godolphin was given to many of their descendants. The second son was created Lord Godolphin, and his son eventually became 8th Duke. The 6th Duke from the maternal side inherited the barony of Conyers, which passed with his other baronies heritable by females, on his son's death, to his sister, Charlotte Lane Fox. Her son, Lord Conyers, married the Baroness Darcy de Knayth, leaving two daughters, who shared the baronies of Conyers, Fauconberg and Darcy de Knayth. The two baronesses married Lord Yarborough and the Earl of Powis, so the titles disappeared into those two families.

To this point, the Dukes married heiresses or at least gentry daughters. The 8th Duke of Leeds is said to have married a domestic servant, which could be exaggerating, as she had four names, usually a sign of reasonable status. She was educated too, and tried to establish a link between her husband's ancestors and Leeds Castle in Kent, though this was unlikely. She produced four sons, but they had only two males between them – the 9th Duke and a short-lived cousin. Again, the 9th Duke had four sons, three of whom lived to maturity but produced only one son between them, the 10th Duke, and he too had one son only. The 11th Duke married an American, who obtained a divorce in the USA which he seems not to have regarded as valid, for he never married again, and that was the end of the Dukes of Leeds and all their minor titles.

MANNERS

The family were knights in Etall, Northumberland until Sir Robert Manners in Edward IV's reign married Eleanor de Ros, who became, by the death of her brother, co-heir to the barony of Ros of Hamlake (Helmesley), Yorkshire. Her sisters died, leaving Eleanor Manners with a clear claim and in possession of the grand Belvoir Castle in Rutland. Her son George became Lord de Ros (with other baronies of Vaux and Trusbut) in 1487, and his heir, Thomas, was advanced to Earl of Rutland in 1525; he picked up more manorial land at the Dissolution of the Monasteries, but his estate was still not massive.

His younger son, John, with few personal prospects, aspired to the hand of Dorothy, heiress of the very rich Sir George Vernon of Haddon, 'King of the Peak' from his 30 lordships in Derbyshire. Sir George thought not a lot of this,

ARE WE RELATED?

so the young couple eloped and married. Making the best of a bad job, the family allowed the marriage to stand and the couple settled down at Haddon Hall, living happily ever after. The story caught the public imagination and 'Sweet Dolly Vernon' and her John were much written and sung about.

The senior line continued as Earls of Rutland, though an heiress carried the barony of Ros into the Cecil family for a time, until her heirs ended and the barony reverted to the Manners 6th Earl. But on his death in 1632 it went to his only child, Katherine, Lady de Ros, who married George Villiers, Duke of Buckingham and favourite of James I and Charles I. He was assassinated and their son died childless, so the barony reverted back to the sisters of the 6th Earl, Mrs Tyrwhitt and Lady Willoughby.

The barony remained in abeyance until through a series of heiresses it went to Lady Charlotte Boyle, who married Lord Henry Fitzgerald, son of the Duke of Leinster, but retained her own surname and arms. Two generations later, it was back with heiresses, where it remained until 1983, when at last a son inherited.

The earldom went to John Manners, grandson of Dolly Vernon, whose son, John, cannily supported William III when James II was deposed, and was made Duke of Rutland and Marquess of Granby as a reward, in 1703.

This last title, used by the heir of the current duke, is frequently found on inn signs, for one long-serving Georgian Marquess of Granby was a dedicated traveller, producing a kind of Michelin guide of his time, praising good inns where he stayed and sending visitors to them. He died before his aged father, leaving his son as heir to the title. His younger brother adopted the name of Manners-Sutton (from his maternal inheritance) and a younger son, Charles Manners-Sutton, became Archbishop of Canterbury. His son, Speaker of the House of Commons from 1817 to 1834, was given the usual viscounty and took the title of Viscount Canterbury. The title continued until 1941, when the male heirs ended. A young brother of the Archbishop was Solicitor General and then Lord Chancellor of Ireland, at which point he was created Baron Manners of Foston.

The dukedom continues in the senior line, rather more solidly based than some financially, because the estates include useful deposits of coal and iron. One Duke happily proclaimed that he owned Belvoir Castle and Haddon Hall, 18,000 acres, extensive mineral deposits in Rutland and Derbyshire, and the magnificently furnished picture gallery at Belvoir.

GROSVENOR

Gros Venor (or Gros venator, originally) means great hunter, and this remained the family claim to distinction for centuries in Cheshire. They bought one of the first baronetcies, in 1621 and jogged along quite happily at Eaton Hall. Then young Sir Thomas went off to London as an MP, and struck up an acquaintance with Master Alexander Davis, a market gardener on a grand scale, who lived down the road in Ebury Fields, which was then open land within a few minutes' walk of the Palace of Westminster. Mr Davis had an only daughter, Mary, who fell for the young Cheshire gentleman, and in 1677 they married, which was considered a bit of a *mésalliance*, though the large dowry of money and land was welcome to a comparatively poor man like Sir Thomas, whose family was impoverished by support for the king.

Sarcastic remarks were made about 'Miss Davis's cabbage patch', but within a generation, Westminster began to expand, and people realised that the Grosvenors were sitting on some very desirable real estate, in the most prestigious developing area in London, named Belgravia after the minor title of Viscount Belgrave.

Mary Davis's grandson became Earl Grosvenor and Viscount Belgrave, her great-grandson, Robert, Marquess of Westminster. Robert also made a marriage which turned out better (socially) than it looked. His bride, Eleanor Egerton, was the daughter of a baronet who inherited, by the deaths of all intervening heirs, the right to the old barony of Grey de Wilton. He was created Earl of Wilton and Eleanor was his only surviving child, so the earldom was remaindered to her younger son, who adopted the name of Egerton.

So Robert and Eleanor's three sons were the 2nd Marquess of Westminster, the Earl of Wilton and Baron Ebury. The 2nd Marquess's son, Hugh Lupus Grosvenor, married the daughter of the Duke of Sutherland, and was made up to Duke of Westminster (most of which he owned) and his brother became Baron Stalbridge.

Queen Victoria was godmother to Hugh Lupus's son, Victor Alexander, Earl Grosvenor, in 1853. The names were male versions of hers (Alexandrina Victoria) but also remembered worthy Mr Davis, whose cabbage patch was the foundation of the great fortune of the Grosvenors. They eventually owned 600 acres in London, immensely valuable, as well as 30,000 acres in Cheshire and Flint, and an estate in Scotland.

ARE WE RELATED?

The family was involved in a resounding scandal in 1770, when Henrietta (Vernon), wife of the 1st Earl, was accused by her husband of adultery with the Duke of Cumberland, son of George II. Agents were employed to follow them, and the couple were caught *in flagrante* in an inn at St Albans. However, Henrietta conducted a spirited defence, which involved bringing various prostitutes to witness that poor Lord Grosvenor was a regular customer, and was vicious, lewd and debauched. Mutual guilt was proved, making it impossible for them to divorce. The marriage continued, uneasily, for thirty more years, until Richard Grosvenor died on 5th August 1802. Henrietta, rising 60, showed what she thought of him by remarrying five weeks later, on 15th September to George, Baron de Hochpied. This was not the last divorce in the family, but the prize, if any, must be claimed by the 2nd Duke, Hugh Richard Grosvenor, who married four times, and divorced three wives. The settlements were huge, on a scale that only the richest duke in England could have afforded. His only son died very young, and his two daughters could not inherit, so the dukedom went to a cousin, descended from the 1st Duke, who nobly maintains against would-be developers the rights of poorer persons to homes in Westminster whose freehold he owns.

There are many Grosvenors descended from further back in the family, especially during the period when they were based in Cheshire, as well as the peers mentioned. However, there may be other huntsmen who were locally reputed as 'great' in their day. Certainly, a family of prominent carpet manufacturers in Kidderminster shared the name.

There are also descents through daughters in the Sankey, Vernon, Shaw-Stewart, Frank, Campbell and Guest families, as well as most of the peerage in England – not bad for a gardener's family.

CHAPTER 6

FAMOUS MEN AND WOMEN

SHAKESPEARE

If you have ancestors named Shakespeare, someone is sure to say 'oh, related to William, I suppose', or even 'descended from William'. And the guess can harden into a 'fact'.

But no one called Shakespeare is descended from William Shakespeare (1564 – 1616). He married Anne Hathaway, rather later than he should have done, in 1582, and their first child, Susanna, arrived six months later; then less than two years later, they had twins, Hamnet and Judith, of whom the boy died aged twelve in 1596. There were no more children after that. Despite his status as an increasingly wealthy man, his daughters were not snapped up early. Susanna married at 24 to Dr John Hall. They had one daughter, Elizabeth, who married first Thomas Nash and after his death in 1646, Sir John Barnard. Dr John died in 1635, his widow in 1649. Shakespeare's younger daughter, Judith, married Thomas Quiney at 31 and had one son, Shakespeare Quiney, who died a few months later in 1617. The death of childless Lady Barnard in 1669 marked the end of the immediate family of William Shakespeare.

William himself was the eldest son of eight children of John Shakespeare and Mary (née Arden). Three sisters died young; the other died unmarried in 1646. There were three brothers, Gilbert, Richard and Edmund, who lived to be young adults; two died in their late twenties, childless. When Richard died in 1613, he is noted as 'last of the brothers of William Shakespeare'.

John Shakespeare (died 1601), William's father, had at least one brother, Henry, who was in financial difficulties in 1582. He is not heard of after that and

59

ARE WE RELATED?

possibly died the next year. So although the name Shakespeare is quite a common one in Warwickshire, none of these Shakespeares will be close kin of the playwright, and any relationship would have to date back beyond about 1520.

NELSON

No one called Nelson is descended from Horatio Nelson, the great Admiral. His marriage to the rich widow Fanny Woolward (Mrs Nisbet) was childless, even before it broke up. Nelson was given a peerage as Baron and then Viscount Nelson of the Nile, and the Sicilian title of Duke of Bronte. By 'special remainder' his designated heirs to the English peerages were his brother and his male heirs, failing whom, the male heirs of his two sisters, Mrs Susannah Bolton and Mrs Catherine Matcham. His brother, the Rev. William Nelson, duly became Viscount Nelson after Trafalgar, and was advanced to Earl Nelson of Trafalgar and Viscount Merton, in gratitude for the dead hero's victory. William's only son, Horatio, died young three years later. There was a daughter, Charlotte, who inherited as Duchess of Bronte, and married the son of another naval hero, Admiral Hood. Samuel Hood inherited his other uncle's title of Viscount Bridport, and their descendants adopted the name of Nelson-Hood.

Meanwhile, on the death of Earl Nelson in 1835, Horatio Nelson's English titles went, according to remainder, to the male heirs of their eldest married sister, Susannah and her husband, Thomas Bolton of Wells, Norfolk. There was only one surviving son, Thomas Bolton too, so in 1835 he adopted the name and arms of Nelson, and inherited the title. He had already produced four sons and a fifth was imminent, so the succession looked safe. Two sons died young, but that left three. The eldest son, Horatio, became 3rd Earl Nelson, and had five sons. Three died before him; the 4th Earl never married and his brother, the 5th Earl, lived to nearly 90. The eldest son, already 60, became 6th Earl, but was childless. He had four brothers and the third brother had a son, but the line ran out again with the 8th Earl in 1981. The heir now was the fifth son's son, Peter John Horatio Nelson. You can imagine that the young man had hardly expected to succeed to the title, at that far remove, so he was pursuing a career, and when unexpectedly called to the peerage was a detective sergeant in the Hertfordshire Police.

Sgt Lord Nelson (who probably got a lot of teasing), has a son and heir (Viscount Merton), and, though the families of the four younger sons of Thomas (Bolton) Nelson had dwindled to one great grandson by 1935, it will probably be a while before the descendants of Catherine Matcham get a look in – but she had three surviving sons (of seven), and a number of grandsons (some known as Eyre-Matcham), so the more distant succession should be amply provided for.

There was also an illegitimate daughter, Horatia, by Lady Hamilton, who was parked with a minder, Mrs Gibson, and is coyly named in Nelson's will as his 'ward Horatia Nelson Thompson'. She married a curate, the Rev. Philip Ward, and had nine children, who would never be in line for a title or estates, but are indubitably of Nelson's blood, if Lady Hamilton was telling the truth about her paternity. Nelson believed her, some of his officers didn't.

There were Nelsons from the generations earlier than the Admiral who may have descendants. They were mainly Norfolk men. Thomas Nelson settled in Kings Lynn by the very early 1600s, and there were descendants in Holme, Scarning, Wendling and Dunham. They were modestly comfortable, with enough money to educate sons and put them into the Church. It was logical that Rev. Edmund Nelson (1722 – 1802) should marry another senior clergyman's daughter, Mary Suckling. Edmund personally was not ambitious, remaining as Rector of Burnham Thorpe for many years, but the name helped his children.

Uncle Capt. Maurice Suckling placed the second boy in the navy and helped a couple of the Nelson cousins too. Two other sons followed their father into the Church. The eldest boy drew on further family connections. Mary Suckling's grandmother was the sister of Sir Robert Walpole, the Prime Minister, and he found places for all his kin in government offices. Only the eldest son, Maurice Nelson, was old enough to benefit by this, when a kinsman got him a position in the navy office, but there may have been relatives still in the civil service who helped young Horatio's career in its early stages. There was a whole collection of clerical cousins named Nelson; the daughters of the family also favoured naval men and there may be kin named Bendysshe, Davies, Blanckley, Moore, Pettiward and McAusland.

WELLINGTON

The family name of the great Duke of Wellington was (at the time) Wellesley, and his own descendants and immediate ancestors are set out in detail in *Burke's*

ARE WE RELATED?

Peerage. His brother Gerald, Earl of Mornington, and created Marquess Wellesley on the strength of his own military achievements, is included, but in older editions not his children, for he did not get around to marrying his lady, Hyacinthe Roland, until after most of them were born. However, they were recognised as his children and accepted in polite society, and one of them, Anne Wellesley, married in 1816 Lt Col. William Cavendish Bentinck, grandson of the Duke of Portland; their granddaughter, Nina Cavendish-Bentinck, married the Earl of Strathmore and her daughter was the Queen Mother. Nina's first cousin got the title of Duke of Portland, and we got Lady Elizabeth Bowes-Lyon as an exemplary queen-consort.

Although the name then was really Wesley, even though respelled as Wellesley, it is unsafe to assume that bearers of the name Wesley are related, since the original family name was Cowley. The first two Cowley ancestors were sent in as spies on the subversive Irish earls. They adopted the name Colley and lived in Castle Carbery and Edenderry. Dudley Colley of Castle Carbery had a daughter, Elizabeth, who married Garret Wesley of Dangan, and her son, dying without heirs, left his property to his cousin, Richard Colley, who had cannily called his eldest son Garret and who legally adopted the name Wesley, becoming 1st Baron Mornington. Garret was promoted to Earl of Mornington and Viscount Wellesley (so they upgraded the surname at that time). Garret's eldest son, Richard, became Lord Mornington and Marquess of Wellesley, but left no legitimate heirs, so the next brother got the Mornington title and the viscounty (from his father) but not his brother's marquessate. This line continued for two more generations, until the males died out.

Meanwhile, Garret, Lord Mornington's third son, young Arthur, put into the army as many younger sons were, was doing rather well in India, and then in the Peninsular Wars. He was created Baron Douro, and then Viscount Wellington of Talavera (after two of his famous victories) in 1809, Earl and Marquess of Wellington in 1812 and Duke of Wellington in 1814. The grateful Spanish king made him Count Vimiera, Duke of Cuidad Regal and Vittoria and Marquis of Torres Vedras, and later he was Prince of Waterloo, with a host of minor orders from all over Europe. Returning home, he held civilian post as Governor of the Royal Military College, Lord Warden of the Cinque Ports, Chief Ranger of Hyde Park, etc. but eventually, disgusted by the mess civilians were making of running the country, he entered politics and became Prime Minister. This was rather a mistake, and even his personal popularity could not carry through his most unpopular measures unopposed.

From the 'Iron Duke' onwards, the descendants are detailed in the *Peerage* under Dukes of Wellington. His younger brother, Rev. Gerald Valerian Wellesley, became a royal chaplain and left a number of descendants, also well documented. The baby of the family, Henry Wellesley, carved out a career for himself as an MP and then a diplomat, being ambassador to Spain, Italy and France (the last after his brother had defeated Napoleon finally). He was rewarded with a barony, and chose to be known by the old family name, as Cowley. Lord Cowley's descendants are also detailed in the peerage volumes.

Further back, before the name Wesley (later Wellesley) was adopted, Garret had sisters only; his father had one brother who left no surviving sons. Dudley Colley, however (father of Elizabeth Wesley), had eight sons and seven daughters, of whom only the eldest son, Henry, is named, and four of the girls. In the generation above, four sons are unnamed. Obviously, there is scope for a relationship here, though proving it, given the deficiencies in Irish records, could be difficult. Some Irish gentry families have been followed up in detail by past genealogists, but the Colleys were fairly small beer at Castle Carbery until the daughter made her fortunate marriage to young Wesley of Dangan.

Incidentally, the Castle Carbery which was the home of the Colleys was in Kildare, while Carbery, from which the Evans (later Evans-Freke) family took their title of Baron Carbery much later, was in Cork. It is this line which produced the Lord Carbery later well known in Kenya as being involved in the unsavoury wife-swapping antics characterised in *White Mischief*, On the more positive side, he and his third wife, June, financed the solo flier Beryl Markham, who was the first woman to fly the Atlantic east to west, in a flimsy plane which just made it before crashing in a swamp.

It is much more likely that you will be able to show a connection of an 'ordinary' family with one of the many peerage families which attained greatness late in the day, through personal merit rather than conquest in battle. There were many peers whose fortunes and titles date from the Industrial Revolution of the 1780s onwards.

ARE WE RELATED?

PEEL

The Peels were yeoman farmers, of Hole House and Peele Fold in Oswaldtwistle, Lancashire. Peele Fold, naturally, always went to the eldest son, so it was up to the others to create their own opportunities. Young Robert Peel (father of the famous Sir Robert) was a third son, and though he delayed marriage until he was 33, his wife soon started producing six boys and three girls (with others who died). Something had to be done.

Cotton textiles were the thing locally, and Robert decided he could design a better system of dyeing and printing patterns on cloth. Endless soggy experiments filled Mrs Peel's kitchen, until finally he got it right, opened a workshop and was soon making a lot of money. By the time the boys were growing, he was able to send them all to good schools, and when he was 50, he was created a baronet. He must have been proud of his boys, all of whom did well – though not one working with his hands in the mill to which they owed their start in life. Two became army officers, one a clergyman, most of them leisured gentlemen. The two eldest sons became Members of Parliament and the eldest, Sir Robert Peel, was a great orator and an accomplished Prime Minister in 1834–5 and 1841–6. It was during his earlier spell as Home Secretary that he set up the Metropolitan Police Force, known for that reason as Peelers.

The sons of Sir Robert Peel MP had distinguished careers, in diplomacy, the army, the navy and politics, and the most accomplished was the fifth, Arthur Wellesley, named after Peel's friend the Duke of Wellington; he served in various ministerial offices and became Viscount Peel, and his son Earl Peel. There must be numerous descendants of the earlier, pre-baronetcy, generations. One branch, descended from a Dr George Peel, settled in South Carolina, and others in South Africa and Canada.

Other industrial giants in their time attained lesser heights. Matthew **Boulton** FRS (1728 – 1809), owner of the Soho Works in Birmingham, became a gentleman, with arms to prove it, and bought a manor house in Oxfordshire; he married Anne Robinson of Lichfield, whose mother was kin to the celebrated Macaulays. His partner and friend James **Watt**, engineer and inventor of many improvements in the use of steam, left no estate or known gentry family, but is remembered in the forename which was used in the Boulton family.

Jedediah **Strutt**, cotton spinner and improver of the stocking frame, came from a yeoman family in South Normanton, Derbyshire, and his grandson attained the title of Baron Belper. His partner, Sir Richard **Arkwright** (1732 – 92) born in Preston, Lancashire, inventor of the improved spinning frame, obtained a personal knighthood and an estate near Chesterfield, but although a number of his grandsons were MPs, with estates of their own, they were not knighted.

Alfred, Lord **Tennyson,** (1809 – 92) the great Victorian poet, came from a somewhat higher level of society, so that his elder brother had a distant claim to the estates of an extinct earldom, though someone else got the title. Their father was a clergyman, and rather unworldly.

Tennyson's ancestors came originally from Preston, Yorkshire, but were well settled in Lincolnshire before Alfred was born, and he himself settled in the Isle of Wight, near his beloved queen. He was rewarded with a barony in 1884, and, although he is unfashionable now, he was really rather a good writer, and enormously prolific. His son, Hallam, had close associations with Australia, and was first Governor General in 1902. His grandson, Lionel, was a well known test match cricketer and wrote verse – but not a patch on his grandfather's.

FLORENCE NIGHTINGALE

Florence Nightingale's exploits in the Crimea as the 'Lady with the lamp' and her subsequent setting up of schools which made nursing into a profession, rather than glorified housework with added blood, are well documented. However, if your name is Nightingale, you are probably not related.

She never married, although she had an offer from Sir Harry Verney, who admired her achievements greatly. He sent to her house in South Street a proposal, beginning 'Dear Miss Nightingale'. But Florence had an elder unmarried

Miss Florence Nightingale

sister, Parthenope, who was by social usage 'Miss' Nightingale, while Florence was 'Miss Florence'. Parthe opened the letter and accepted the proposal. There was nothing to be done; Sir Harry married her, in 1858, telling his son she was in her fortieth year, a lady, but without the beauty of her sister, and although Florence spent a lot of her time down at their Buckingham mansion, Claydon House, there was never a hint of 'goings on'. Only Sir Harry's butler was told, and probably other servants guessed what had been intended.

The father of the two girls was originally named William Edward Shore (1794 – 1874), son of a Sheffield banker, William Shore, who had married Mary Evans, daughter of George Evans of Cromford, Derby, and his wife Anne, only sister of Peter Nightingale of Lea and Woodend. When the Nightingale line died out, Peter's property came to his great niece, Mrs Shore. Her husband, taking possession as married men were then entitled to do, retired from banking and bought a nice little estate at Embley, Hampshire adopting the name Nightingale. For some time, the couple travelled in Italy, where Frances Parthenope was born at Naples (and given its classical nickname as her christian name) and Florence was borne at Firenze (in English, Florence).

Hundreds of little girls were named after their parents' heroine, in the next fifty years after the Crimea, but neither sister had any children. The closest kin could be descended from Mary Shore, sister of William Edward Nightingale, who married Samuel Smith of Parndon, Essex, the brother of Florence's mother, Frances. The senior line of the Shore family continued at Norton Hall, Derbyshire. The Smith sisters married into the families of Nicholson and Bonham-Carter.

ELIZABETH GARRETT ANDERSON

Elizabeth Garrett Anderson was the first qualified woman doctor in England. Her ancestors had never been content to stay put. An early gunsmith ancestor, Harmon Garrett, went to America and founded Lancaster, Pennsylvania in 1636, but returned home in 1660 to Wickham Market. A younger son, Richard, became a scythe manufacturer in Leiston, Suffolk, from where his youngest son, Newson, went to London and married in 1834 Louisa Dunnell, also of a Suffolk family.

Newson managed pawnbrokers' shops for her well-to-do father in London, but in 1841, took his young family to healthier Snape, at Aldeburgh, and prospered as a coal and corn merchant. He then started malting, and built up a fleet of ships to carry goods, owned a brickyard, gasworks and developed estates of houses. By 1850, he was a rich man, and built himself a mansion, Alde House (later his daughter's home). His rivalry was great with his elder brother, Richard, whose agricultural machinery business was equally successful, and he quarrelled with the vicar, the bailiff (mayor) and other merchants. No wonder his daughter was wilful.

Elizabeth Garrett was the second daughter of Newson and Louisa Garrett and was born in Whitechapel in 1836. She was given the usual sort of education for a girl at the time. She was taught by a governess, then at a private school in Blackheath, to 'finish' her, ready to be a young lady

Elizabeth Garrett

of fashion, trained to be a nice, submissive wife. Much to her father's astonishment, his little dove turned out to be a hawk, learning Latin and arithmetic from her brothers' tutor, and making friends with Emily Davies, later the founder of Girton College. In 1859, enthused by the visit to England by Elizabeth Blackwell, an American doctor, she expressed an unseemly interest in medicine herself. Her parents were horrified, but, being rich, they had connections which allowed her to sit in on a few lectures at the Middlesex Hospital, which were supposed to frighten her off. They didn't, and the medical students, who at first thought it was fun to have a pretty, young red-head around, protested vigorously that it was totally unsuitable for a female to be there when they were dissecting. Ladies were not supposed to know about bodies, especially not male bodies. And she was altogether too clever. She was refused admission to training, so went to Scotland, where they were a little less sexist, but even here, opposition hardened. After years of struggling with the system, she was allowed to take the Licentiate of the Society of Apothecaries, but for her full MB, she had to go to the Sorbonne in Paris.

ARE WE RELATED?

Returning home, she continued to fight for the right of women to become doctors, setting up a medical school to ease their training, thus enabling many other women to follow in her footsteps (144 by 1892). She also set up a dispensary for poor women and children, where she worked untiringly. Later she raised money for a New Hospital for Women (later the Elizabeth Garrett Anderson Hospital). She also topped the poll for the first elected London School Board, in 1860, and was first and, for a long time, the only female member of the BMA.

She was able to do more or less what she wanted, because at 36, she married a wealthy ship owner, James Skelton Anderson, high-achieving son of a poor clergyman, the Rev. Alexander Anderson, who gave her his full financial and moral support. Her children, Louisa and Alan (and Margaret, who died young), were cared for at their home in Upper Berkeley Street by half a dozen servants, half Scots, half from Suffolk, and grew up to follow in their parents' footsteps. Alan built ships and was knighted for his work as Controller of the Navy, in 1917, just before his mother died. His sister, Louisa Garrett Anderson, became an eminent doctor and a militant suffragette. She was chief surgeon to the military hospital in Endell Street and set up hospitals in France in the Great War, terrifying any general into co-operation.

In her old age, Dr Elizabeth Garrett Anderson retired to Aldeburgh, where she succeeded her venerable father and her husband as Mayor, the first woman to hold office, though she never received the national honours she richly deserved. She died leaving her two children and four grandchildren from Alan's marriage. Her four brothers Edmund, Newson, Samuel and George, left descendants, alone with her sisters, Louisa (Mrs James Smith), Alice (Mrs Philip Cowell), Millicent (Mrs Henry Fawcett), Agnes, and Josephine, who between them produced numerous children.

Elizabeth had been courted by Henry Fawcett, the blind Professor of Political Economy at Cambridge. She was still training and turned him down, but she was not pleased when he married her younger sister, Millicent, in 1887. Millicent Fawcett, supported by Henry, now Postmaster General, became leader of the National Union of Women's Suffrage Societies, the more acceptable face of the movement for votes for women, using intellectual arguments and networking, rather than smashing windows and throwing bombs. Elizabeth had been, first, a militant WPSU supporter, which worried her gentler sister. Millicent lived to see the success of her campaign, and died a Dame of the British Empire; the Fawcett Society, cradle of 'the Women's Movement', is named after her.

ADA AUGUSTA NOEL BYRON, COUNTESS OF LOVELACE 1816–52

Ada was a popular late Victorian name, mainly given to aunts of more than usually plain aspect, though the original Ada was an absolute stunner. This was Lord Byron's daughter, the only child of his unhappy marriage to Anna Isabella Milbanke.

Lord Byron in a costume he bought on a trip to Greece in 1809

He had recently written *The Giaour*, and his beautiful heroine, full of eastern promise, was Adah, so the name was given to the baby, who developed into a black ringleted, dark-eyed glamour girl, looking startlingly eastern. Her classical beauty was her mother's, enhanced by her father's less regular and wild, romantic looks. They had the same tumbling curls and the same rather wild nature, but Ada was restrained by her mother and grandmother, Judith Noel. Her more cerebral rebellion came after she had escaped to early marriage with handsome, young William, Lord King, and, as she had inherited a claim to the barony of Wentworth through her mother, he was created Earl of Lovelace.

Ada's rebellion did not follow the paternal pattern of sexual aberration, which included incest with his half sister, Augusta Leigh. She began a lifelong affair with mathematics, which brought her into close friendship with the archetypal computer nerd, Charles Babbage, inventor of the first calculating engine. Together, she and Babbage enthused over numbers, making useful advances in the fledgling applied science. However, one of the ways they applied it was to devise an 'infallible' system for betting on horses, which was predictably unsuccessful, and lost Lady Lovelace a lot of money.

Ada had three children: Anne, Byron Noel-King and Ralph Gordon Noel-King, both boys becoming Barons Wentworth in turn. Ralph followed his father as 2nd Lord Lovelace and had an only daughter, Ada Mary, Baroness Wentworth (who died unmarried in 1917). The heir was her venerable aunt Anne, who had married Wilfred Scawen Blunt, the well-known poet. Anne died within six months, leaving her only daughter, Judith (Mrs Lytton) as Baroness Wentworth. Judith Blunt-Lytton, famous as an Arab horse breeder (the Crabbet Stud) divorced her husband (later Earl of Lytton), and with her children adopted the name Lytton-Milbanke. Her heir was therefore Noel Scawen Lytton-Milbanke (Lord Lytton and Lord Wentworth) with two major poets, the distinguished historical novelist and politician, Edward Bulwer Lytton, and more distantly, Lord Clarendon, the Stuart historian, in his lineage.

There were a few illegitimate siblings, including Allegra, by Claire Clairmont, who died as a child, and Byron's daughter by Augusta Leigh, and possibly others by his Italian mistress, but no legitimate siblings. The next Lord Byron was his cousin, also George, and there are numerous kin on this side of the family.

Emmeline Pankhurst (1858 – 1928)

Mrs Pankhurst is the embodiment of the militant suffrage movement. Born Emmeline Goulden, pampered eldest child of a calico printer, Robert Goulden, of Manchester, she was sent to school in Paris, where she got 'fancy ideas' that women had rights to their own property and to voting on the same basis as men.

Emmeline Pankhurst

At 21, she returned and married her father's friend, Dr Richard Marsden Pankhurst, 22 years her senior, with a comfortable lifestyle in Stretford, a somewhat 'better' area of Manchester than Pendleton, where the Gouldens had lived. She and Dr Pankhurst (who was a PhD and a barrister, not a medical man) were on the committee for reform of the Married Women's Property Act, which was successful, then turned to supporting female suffrage. They moved to London for a time, where Emmeline promoted the Women's Suffrage League, joined the Match Girls' Strike and became a member of the Independent Labour Party, as well as giving birth to three of her five children. Returning to Manchester in 1893, Dr Pankhurst stood for Parliment on the suffrage issue, but was advised to go home and keep his wife in order. He died of pneumonia, five years later, developed from a cold caught on the hustings.

ARE WE RELATED?

As a widow, Emmeline became Registrar of births and deaths in Chorlton on Medlock, but was asked to resign because of her political activism. Two of her daughters, the spoilt beauty, Christabel, and the more sensible and practical Sylvia, joined her in the suffrage movement, forming the Women's Social and Political Union, and Christabel encouraged her mother to turn militant. This involved disrupting political meetings, throwing stones through windows, setting bombs in politicians' houses, and chaining themselves to railings. The WSPU members were often sent to prison, where they refused to eat. When they became weak, they were released only to be re-imprisoned when they recovered (under the 'Cat and Mouse' Act), and then forcibly fed with tubes. Their tactics made them appear faintly ridiculous and dangerous, though attention-grabbing, and undermined the work done by the rival organisation (NUWSS) under Millicent Fawcett, which sought to persuade MPs that women were sensible people.

The outbreak of war in 1914 saw an end to the violent demonstrations. Emmeline and Christabel donned glamorous frocks and went on recruiting drives, handing white feathers to any young men not serving. Sylvia, hating the war, broke away and organised soup kitchens in the East End, and taught the wives of soldiers domestic skills and how to manage budgets. The good service given by many young women in the war forced recognition of their status, and women over 30 were given votes in 1919, on almost the same terms as men, though general adult suffrage was not given till 1928. Emmeline then stood for Parliament as a Conservative, though in a hopeless seat, Christabel went in for fringe religions and Sylvia was imprisoned as a Communist. At 45, she had an illegitimate son, Richard.

There are likely to be Goulden relatives in the Manchester area, where they were deep-rooted, since Emmeline had at least four brothers and a sister. The name Richard Goulden runs in the family, which is that of a well-known comic actor of the 1940 – 60 period. There may also be Pankhursts in Stoke-on-Trent, Staffordshire, since Emmeline's husband had at least one brother, John Calvin Pankhurst, who went to America. There are also Manx connections, since Emmeline's mother was from the Isle of Man.

CHAPTER 7

A COAT OF ARMS?

Some people, instead of asking 'Who are my ancestors?' demand to have 'the family coat of arms'. Most people simply have not got one. And even if you find that there are arms belonging to a person named Bloggs, it doesn't mean that everyone called Bloggs can use it. Too many people fall for the arms' pedlars, who advertise that they will find 'your' coat of arms and sell you a parchmentised scroll with it on (or even a nicely framed picture) with a history of the name, all for a fee, of course. If they can't find arms for anyone with your surname, the next name in the alphabetical list will do.

There is no such thing as a 'family coat of arms' or a general right which applies to everyone bearing that surname. Only the person to whom the arms were granted in the first place and his immediate male descendants are really entitled to those arms. His brother's descendants could make a good case for having a coat of arms issued which is very similar, with some slight variation to show they are not his own descendants, but no one else bearing that name is entitled to display the arms at all. The sole heiress of an arms-bearer can convey the right to use his arms to her children.

Some people refer to 'the family crest', as if this was another name for arms. The crest is the device which sits on top of the whole set-up when arms are represented on a shield shape, surmounted by a helmet which shows the 'degree' of the owner of the arms. A closed helmet in profile is used by an untitled gentleman; a helmet front facing with open visor for a baronet; a profile helmet with five open bars for a baron, earl, etc.; and a full face helmet with six open bars gilded for royalty. The helmet is surmounted by a striped line, representing a roll of twisted silk, and on top will be an animal (or section of one), a plant,

ARE WE RELATED?

etc. This is likely to be one of the devices of the shield, such as a demi-lion, a hunting dog, a tree, a ship. The Counts of Anjou had a sprig of broom (*planta genista*) in their helmets, and this gave its name to the whole dynasty, as Plantagenet. Small personal objects like cuff-links may only have room for the crest, and this is probably how the confusion arose between arms and crest.

If you use someone else's arms in a place where the public can see them, you could in theory be visited by the officers of the College of Heralds, who would be entitled to rip down the offending display, whether it was on your mantelpiece, your gate, your car, or, presumably, embroidered on fabric and worn as a dress. They are not known to have taken such a public action recently, though less than a hundred years ago a Buckinghamshire resident was heavily fined for displaying on her carriage the arms of Vivian, to which she was not entitled. The social embarrassment which this caused made her leave the county. Lord Lyon, the principal Heraldic Officer in Scotland, is fiercer and you have to 'matriculate' (register) even the genuine right to arms.

Coats of arms had a practical purpose in medieval times: they were embroidered on cloth to wear over full suits of armour, so that when the helmet was closed, the knight could be recognised in battle as 'one of ours' before those on the same side had hacked him to pieces. 'Oops, sorry, Thomas mate' was no substitute. His retainers, squires, pages, etc. wore the same arms, his banners and shields displayed them, and his castle gates, and eventually his tomb, showed the same devices. The older a coat of arms is, the simpler the appearance: a single plain colour, or one red lion on a white (silver) background. Once the simple combinations had been used up, later arms were more complex and fussy.

Marriage of an arms-bearer (also known as an *armiger*) to the only daughter of another armiger entitled him to display her father's arms with his own, and by the time there had been several marriages to heiresses, the number of arms quartered by their descendants meant division and subdivision of the shield. Sixteen quarters was what you aimed at – showing any more on semi-formal occasions was considered a bit flashy. Sixty-four resulted in an impressive but messy mixture of tiny heraldic devices. In 1904 Mr Henry Crampton Lloyd had 356, though with a great deal of repetition.

However, the real heyday of arms possession came after the days when most gentlemen who used them were likely to be out there fighting in armour. The right to issue arms, and make sure that no two persons had precisely the same ones, was vested in the College of Arms, whose staff consisted of the Kings of Arms and the various pursuivants and heralds.

The early heralds were not above massaging the facts to make the rich sheep farmers and merchants seem to have a connection with an old baronial family, preferably one which had died out, so there was no come-back. And 'improvement' of surnames was in order. Herald Tom Risley 'discovered' that he was really Thomas Wriothesley, which sounded far better for a man whose son became Earl of Southampton. The Smiths forsook their honest trading connections to become Smythes, and one Smith 'discovered' he was descended from a mythical medieval knight named de Carrington. However, one of Lord Carrington's cousins resolutely refused to change his name, and Abel Smith's son won the jackpot by marrying a princess of sorts – though she was adamant that she should be known as Lady May Abel-Smith.

The later the arms, the more complicated they are likely to be – witness the Rothschild arms, with five arrows for the five sons who dispersed over Europe and made their fortunes, an imperial spread eagle, a British Lion rampant, a red spiked shield (punning on 'rot schild') and no less than three crests – the eagle again, the Prince of Wales's triple feathers (for the two masters most usefully served), and a pair of buffalo horns with a mullet (star shape) in between (the significance of these horns is in some doubt – they are possibly Wotan-style horns, possibly badly drawn wings, for Frankfort). There are also supporters on either side of the shield, holding it up: the lion and unicorn as in the English royal arms.

The Rothschild arms.

ARE WE RELATED?

When a father dies, his eldest son inherits the actual family coat of arms. In his lifetime, the son may display the arms with a 'label' (a sort of inverted comb shape). If the younger sons want to use the arms, they must add a 'cadency mark' to show that they are not the eldest. Each son's mark shows his own position in the family, and their sons have marks on top of their father's mark.

Line of Cadency Marks.

The Heir, or first son, the LABEL

Second son, the CRESCENT

Third Son, the MULLET

Fourth Son, the MARTLET

Fifth Son, the ANNULET

Sixth Son, the FLEUR-DE-LIS

Seventh Son, the THE ROSE

Eighth Son, the CROSS MOLINE

Ninth Son, the DOUBLE QUATREFOIL

A COAT OF ARMS?

Someone who becomes a baronet has a mark of an open hand, called the Red Hand of Ulster, in the top right-hand corner. This is what would normally be called the top left-hand corner, but the convention is that you are wearing the arms on a shield and looking from behind, so your right is what faces the viewer's left.

Someone who is the illegitimate son of an armiger may be granted the use of arms, with the addition of a wavy border round his father's arms. You will hear that they had a 'bar sinister', which does not exist, but you may find a few old arms 'debruised' with a 'baton sinister', a short diagonal line across the centre of the shield, from top 'left' to bottom 'right'. Mind you, father had to be royal or a very important nobleman, and his son very rich and well known to be a royal bastard for this grant of arms to happen. Charles II was responsible for the production of various illegitimate sons (the Duke of Grafton, the Duke of St Albans, and others) and William IV, when Duke of Clarence, for the FitzClarences (Earls of Munster).

Royal arms with baton sinister for Fitzroy, Duke of Grafton.

The fully displayed arms are generally on a shield shape, with a helmet and crest and mantling (curly bits of framework, representing the long length of cloth which knights in the Crusades used to keep the sun off the backs of their necks). There may be supporters – figures of people or animals on either side of the shield – usually lions or whatever off the shield in old coats of arms, or people who contributed to the wealth and advancement of later peers. For instance, Nelson had a sailor, and Cubbitt, the great builder of London, has a pair of workmen, one with architectural dividers and one with a tamper, for bricklayer or paviour.

ARE WE RELATED?

The Nelson arms. These include the waves of the sea, a disabled ship, a palm tree and a fort in ruins, three bombs, the crest of a naval crown and the stem of a Spanish galleon; the supporters are a Victorian sailor and a lion with two pieces of broken flagstaff bearing a Spanish flag.

The arms of Cubbitt, the London builder, showing two workmen as supporters.

Even if arms have been in your family for 'donkey's years', on a heraldic box, china, silver, painting or bookplate, it is not absolute proof of your entitlement. It may be that your great-grandfather fell for one of the arms pedlars in Victorian times, or even that he designed them himself. A lot of Victorian gentlemen with time on their hands did just that, and a few of these arms even appear in books like *Burke's General Armory*, which does not distinguish the genuine from the fake. The authority on genuine arms is Fox-Davies, who listed authentic armigers, and added in a handful of 'arms as used by' a family, where he thought they were most probably genuine, though their origins, and the date of any grant, were lost in the mists of time.

Harris: canting arms, granted by the College of Heralds;
'herisson' is French for hedgehog.

So if you want a coat of arms ...

- Buy one from the arms pedlars, and offer two fingers to the rest. Let the knowledgeable laugh, you don't care. But will your children be embarrassed?

- Buy one, research which family it actually belongs to, and label it as such ('The arms of the Murrays of Tullibardine'), letting people assume you are related. Bit risky if the Earl of Tullibardine or a friend of his drops in for coffee one day.

- Show the arms and admit you are not related, before someone in the know makes a mockery of you.

- Trace your own family and discover whether there was ever an actual coat of arms used by a proven relative, however far back, or however distant the link.

- Design your own.

- Go to the College of Heralds and buy your own authentic coat of arms, for a lot of money. They will research your family tree a little way, to see if they can come up with a link to an armiger, in which case they will give you something similar to an existing coat, 'differenced' by changing the background colour or one of the devices on the shield. If there is no link to an armiger, they check that you are respectable, preferably in a professional

ARE WE RELATED?

position, and rich enough to uphold the dignity of arms, and generally try to equip you with new arms and a crest which refer in some way either to your surname or your career. A naval officer or someone fond of sailing would have a ship or wavy lines representing the sea; a man named Bullock or a cattle breeder, the head of a fierce-looking bull; a wealthy doctor stylised medicine bottles. If you are a scientist, you get an old-style retort shape; if your name is Woodgate, you get a device like a block of timber and a gate; If it is Rose, you get a few roses; if it is Fletcher, you get arrows; if it is Buckle – you've guessed. Think hard if your name is Chambers or Sponge. However, the heraldic devices are pretty stylised and geometric so they are not crude facsimiles of the article in question. The types of arms which play on the name they refer to are called 'canting arms'.

CHAPTER 8

GENTLEMEN AND LADIES-IN-WAITING

Sometimes you will find a marriage certificate which says that the father of groom or bride was a 'gentleman'. This may be true, or it may come from a wish to impress the in-laws, which also caused bank clerks to become bankers and jobbing carpenters building contractors.

Strictly, a gentleman is a man possessed of a coat of arms and an estate, though without a title of any kind. By Victorian times it had become a description applied to anyone who could afford to live without working with his hands. A retired grocer, living on money wisely invested, would describe himself as a gentleman, though his total 'estate' might be a fairly modest house and garden in a suburb of Birmingham. Professional men like barristers could call themselves gentlemen (and might indeed come from that level, since the early stages of the trade require financial support in the background); officers in the army and navy were gentlemen. Those appointed from the ranks in wartime for their abilities, not intending to remain in the regular army, were styled 'temporary gentlemen'. So the Victorian description implied money and leisure, rather than birth and background.

Before 1800, the description was more tightly used, and where found should be regarded as evidence of genuine status. It is true that the great fortunes made in the Industrial Revolution by enterprising weavers, spinners or ironmasters could lead to their sons being regarded as gentlemen, with the advantage of education, grand housing and the lack of any need to involve themselves directly in the business, which would be run by managers. The father would

ARE WE RELATED?

never be regarded as more than 'a self-made man' if he was rich and abrasive, or 'one of nature's gentlemen' if he was rich, generous and properly respectful to his betters (by birth). The great industrialist Titus Salt of Bradford came from 'nowhere' (or, to be precise, Hunslet, Yorkshire) to become not only enormously wealthy and senior Alderman of Bradford, but also the pioneer of model towns to accommodate his workforce in comparative comfort. In 1869 he was given the title of baronet as Salt of Saltaire, his town on the river Aire. His family never did the necessary political intriguing to be 'promoted' further in the scale.

The majority of those described as 'gentlemen', however, had come from a background of some affluence, by birth into an 'old' family. Every family is 'old' in that it has ancestry going back into the mists of time, but in this case, 'old' means with a proven descent from men who were also gentry.

In the English system, this has never precluded men from going into commerce and making money to support a more leisured lifestyle. It was traditional for the eldest son to inherit the family estate (by *primogeniture*) and for the younger ones to be put into as good a trade as the father could afford. In later centuries, this tended to be the army, the navy, the law or the Church (and it was a dean's niece who quoted to me the old aphorism: 'The fool of the family, put him into the Church'). In earlier times, the younger sons were apprenticed as merchants in London and some, like Dick Whittington, a squire's son from Gloucestershire, made a spectacular success, marrying wealth, becoming Lord Mayor and owning a fleet of ships. Many were able to come back to their native county and buy estates which were much larger than those of their eldest brother, founding a line of actual peers.

Others, of course, did not do so well, through ill health, bad luck or lack of application, and the younger sons of these younger sons would very soon slide into the lower reaches of society, though perhaps retaining the knowledge that somewhere, back in time, 'we were gentlemen'. Some even made sure that their sons were educated – at a time when education was largely a matter of paying and money was hard to find.

It is a cliché that Irish bricklayers named O'Brien would throw their mates on the building site into hysterical laughter by proclaiming 'We was Kings in Ireland', though if you go back far enough, it was quite true. Whether the average brickie could prove his descent from Brian Boru is another matter, but it was never impossible that the connection existed.

GENTLEMEN AND LADIES-IN-WAITING

The first check is to look at old volumes of *Burke's Landed Gentry* to see if the family name occurs there. The descent of the main line is fully worked out, but that of the younger sons may say 'and had issue'. If you can trace your family backwards until it coincides with the couple who had this issue, then there may be several proven older generations. It would be risky to assume that where the younger son is merely stated as 'John born 1701' somewhere in the north or west of England, he is identical with your John married in about 1730 in London, though if he uses forenames normal in that family, and seems tolerably affluent, the line is worth investigating closely, through wills of father and brothers. The more rare the surname, the greater the likelihood of a link, and of being able to prove it.

There are authentic gentry families who were not included in *Burke*. The qualification was supposed to be the possession of 1,000 acres of land, not a measly 900; it was obviously easier to achieve in Ireland, where vast stretches of bog contributed size without value, so relatively less affluent families are included (usually in a separate section after the English, Welsh and Scots gentry). An extremly rich man whose property was concentrated in a small area of London might not be included, unless he siphoned off some of his wealth into a country estate (or bought himself a peerage).

All inheritance is subject to vicissitues, so it is entirely possible that the family estate was either gambled away, left between daughters who carried it into some other families, or lost through bad management or a run of bad luck with harvests, which meant that more and more of the land was mortgaged and lost. A great deal of land in the country changed hands between 1795 and 1830, when old families who did not adopt new and more economic methods of cultivation could not run their estates profitably and had to sell to the 'opulent grocers' or arms manufacturers who had made a profit out of the Napoleonic Wars. The process was accelerated at the end of 19th century, when country landowners suffered from imported goods, and often completed in 1919, when the rising prices during the long war (1914 – 18) ruined many aristocrats and forced sales to the war-affluent.

There has always been migration from the country to towns or from England to America (and later to Canada, South Africa, Australia and New Zealand), usually by younger sons, which can result in a total severing of family ties, though a vague memory of the past may be handed down. If those who left kept in touch, their descent is recorded in the *Peerage* or *Landed Gentry*. But most simply did not, and tracing the intervening links may be very difficult, involving a lot of work in the country of migration before there is any hope of establishing a British connection.

In a small number of cases, even of early emigration, sheer greed may have provided the necessary link. For instance, a Henry Woolcott left Somerset in the mid 17th century. He was the son of a farmer then in fairly good circumstances, who gave his son a useful amount of money to buy land in this new country of America, and Henry was content to make over his interest in the farm to his next brother, George. Henry duly invested in land and did remarkably well, while, as it happens, the Somerset farm was embarrassed by the depredations of the Civil War and after. But Henry's son decided that he was the heir of the eldest son, and he wanted the lot; so he commenced litigation for the remnant of the estate back home. The case rumbled on and used up all the money there was left in lawyers' fees.

The descendants of Henry Woolcott, presumably not knowing of this case with its full proof of his origins, blithely claimed, totally incorrectly, that they were related to an armigerous family in Shropshire because they were in the books and the Somerset family were not.

So always check the records of the Court of Chancery, to see whether there is a case indexed as *Bloggs v Bloggs – re land/money*, which may uncover a large amount of the family pedigree and also give sidelights on the (not always admirable) character of your ancestors.

My ancestor was a lady-in-waiting

This story usually goes on '... to Queen Victoria, and she ran away with the coachman/gardener'. If I've heard this once, I heard it hundreds of times, and it has never, sadly, been true.

Ladies-in-waiting were (and are) aristocratic females, almost certainly with one of the surnames listed in the Appendix, who were employed about the court as, so to speak, personal assistants to the queen. The duties consisted of attendance on the queen, smoothing her life in the palace and outside it, carrying gloves, bouquets, parasols or umbrellas, and guarding her from irritation, ill-chosen conversation and non-preselected people. The senior lady would answer non-official, non-family correspondence, usually thanking people for good wishes and passing on congratulations to people who were 100, or had been married 60 years, or whatever. The senior ones, who might be widows or mature wives of male court officials, would be in charge of the younger ones, and watch them like hawks, so their opportunities for dalliance at all, never mind out of their class, would be absolutely minimal. Marriage for them was a matter of alliance with another similar family – the ladies would not have contemplated a liaison with a servant.

If you are sure your ancestor worked for the royal family, then the Royal Archivist at Windsor Castle, Berkshire, will be able to settle it.

Many of these stories seem to have arisen because of confusion between a lady-in-waiting and a lady's maid. The latter attended rich ladies, looked after their clothes, washed the really fine undies, mended tiny tears, laid the dresses out, dressed their mistress, did her hair, undressed her at night, accompanied her on visits, guarding the jewel box, and carried confidential messages. Some were with their ladies for a long time and were much trusted, even becoming as near to friends as you got between the classes.

Lady's maids were servants, even if superior servants, and the time might come when they wished to marry. Because they would have saved up a lot of wages and tips, and have a fine wardrobe of Madam's cast-offs, they were much sought after and might marry a rising tradesman or even a young professional man. Marriage with a gardener or coachman would be reckoned as 'lowering' themselves, which could be where the family story arose. The same applies to rich farmers' daughters. If the marriage didn't work out, because of different standards, there was every temptation for the wife to exaggerate what she had given up for love.

The same applies if the story is that Miss X was a royal dressmaker. If it is true, the archivist will know. But most will turn out to be 'Court' dressmakers, which is not the same. These were people who made clothes, either for London or provincial gentlewomen who were presented at court functions, or who wished they might be. Some women never even came within miles of London, but attended municipal dances in Bristol, or Batley, or Newcastle, and needed gowns to knock the locals for six. Plain Ada Bott could not sell them clothes, but Madame Adelina Bottoni, Court dressmaker, might.

CHAPTER 9

WHAT IF THE CONNECTION IS ILLEGITIMATE?

The family story may claim that your grandfather was the son of the local squire, an earl or even a member of the royal family. Sometimes this is true, sometimes it is a total fantasy. Mostly it is somewhere in between – he was illegitimate, yes; but his father was the butler, the boot boy, or an ordinary labourer.

How do I prove it?

Paradoxically, it is easier to prove the tradition is untrue than that it is true. First, get grandfather's birth certificate. If he is straightforwardly illegitimate, no father will be named on the certificate except in the fairly uncommon event that he accompanied the mother when registering the child. If they lived together at the time, but, for some reason, they could not marry, he may have done this. If a previous marriage had broken down, divorce was not really an option for ordinary folk, since it was so expensive and fraught with legal complications. A 'guilty party' who had left his wife and was living with another woman would normally be unable to get a divorce without her agreement. A woman generally had to prove not just adultery or desertion, but cruelty as well. So many couples regrouped without formality.

If the couple were bold enough, they might even claim to be married, or allow the registrar to imply this, by being economical with the truth. If they were caught in deliberate lies, they could be fined, but honest mistakes might be defended. If two people are named on the certificate, it is likely they were the parents, even if no trace of the marriage can be found.

WHAT IF THE CONNECTION IS ILLEGITIMATE?

The situation of a married woman or young widow who had a child is different. The legal assumption is that the child of a married woman is that of her husband, unless he can prove non-access for at least ten months. If a wife has answered the question 'what is your husband's name?' correctly, it would take a psychic registrar to realise the husband was not the father. True, if he had been dead for four years, realisation might dawn, but not if his death was registered elsewhere. Ladies who looked respectable could get away with a lot.

If a single woman had a child, the pressure from her family and the local authorities would be to name the man and sue for maintenance. An ordinary poor girl in Victorian times was likely to be sent to the workhouse to have the child, which might remain in the workhouse school or children's home. The mother could take the child home, if she had one to go to, but because she was likely to need support from the union, the Poor Law guardians would order her to issue a summons for affiliation and maintenance against the father.

The case would be heard in Petty Sessions, and these records should be available in the local archives, publicly if they are at least 30 years old. Up to about 50 years ago, the local newspaper was also likely to have published at least a brief report with the names involved. The older the case, the more graphic the details since it was at one time necessary for a girl to provide corroborative evidence of a rather private activity. Sometimes this evidence was that he had come to her mother's house or some public place and announced his intention of marrying her; sometimes there were near eye-witness accounts.

Some girls issued a summons and the man hurriedly paid up, to avoid the publicity of a court appearance. The accusation will be noted in the Police Summons Book, and the reason for withdrawing it 'settled out of court'. Sometimes there will be a later variation of the sum agreed to be paid, as the child grows older or the mother marries a man with a good income. Summons books may be in the archives or in a police museum, or even still gathering dust in an old police station's basement.

If the father was rich – and especially if he was rich and married – he was likely to make a settlement for the child before the news became public. In this case, there would be no official record, though some paperwork may exist with a family solicitor and occasionally, such papers from long enough ago have been deposited in archives. It is likely that sensitive papers under a hundred years old will have been weeded, or are not deposited. If so, you have no right of access to private records.

ARE WE RELATED?

If you can prove that the female ancestor was actually a servant in the local gentry house, and the story is that she was taken advantage of by the son of the house (or a named guest), the scenario looks possible. This did happen, since housemaids were part of the facilities for some young men. Check first if she was young and pretty. It is not likely that young gentlemen would bother with a 38-year-old cook with a face like a prison warder. Then check the local paper to see if the young man was actually there during the operative time. If he was serving in India, or on safari in Africa, then another think is required. If the named man was recently married, then possibly he would have been otherwise engaged – unless his wife was pregnant, which was regarded as an excuse for straying.

It was often the case that the rich family would find a husband for the girl, who would take her and the child, with a suitable financial sweetener. Look for a 'late' marriage and a sudden increase in the wealth of a former servant and a labourer, perhaps opening a shop or running a public house. The child would usually be treated pretty well – not only was he or she a source of present riches but a possible future lever against the father. Be aware that the really clever servant girl would sometimes manoeuvre the local squire into this position, then marry the man who was her real sweetheart (and occasionally the real father of the child). Mere late marriage is not proof. Our 38-year-old cook might not appeal to the young squire, but for the gardener her good cooking and her saved-up wages might be quite sufficient, and start them off in a shop, at that.

The appearance of the illegitimate child as an adult may confirm or cast doubt on the story. If his appearance is nothing like that of his siblings, and very close to that of the putative gentry father or his kin, as seen hanging in portraits on the ancestral walls, then there is a case to answer. Do not be carried away by supposed resemblances of a baby to the adult father: half the (well-nourished) babies in the country looked like Winston Churchill in his day. Or perhaps, rather, the mature, bald Winston Churchill often looked like a large baby on the verge of yelling. Look at the ear shape, the nose, the tilt of the eyebrow – these are the permanent features. DNA testing is now another possibility, but you have to get the other party to agree, which could be difficult. Occasionally, there is a family resemblance which causes talk – but the link is through an earlier generation, when the wicked squire did really take advantage of the young maiden.

There is generally talk in the village anyway, which may have been committed to paper by some writer. In a local village, there was a story that the lord of the manor, Thomas Francis Fremantle, was the father of at least one child who was by name the son of a local farmer. The undoubted fact that the squire sent the young man to university and was frequently and successfully asked to pay his debts does rather suggest either extreme benevolence or some truth in the story.

It is always worth looking at the will of the putative father for any reference to 'William son of Mary Jones, late my servant', or 'the child known as William Bloggs, son of Jane now the wife of Edward Bloggs'. This type of reference declines as Victorian morality sets in, though it may be replaced by a sum of money given to a solicitor 'in trust for purposes arranged'.

Before 1834, all poor relief was handled by the parish itself, and this would normally involve the maintenance of illegitimate children. The parish Overseers of the Poor were in charge of this, and their first step, on spotting a pregnant girl, was to ask her who the father was. Often this was a formality, since few secrets are kept in a small village. The named man was then brought before them and offered the opportunity to marry the girl, if necessary with help in finding a cottage. He could also deny the charge, in which case he was sent to gaol to await the hearing of the case (unless his family provided a bond for his appearance). If he agreed the claim but did not intend to marry the girl he had to sign a bastardy bond to pay for the lying-in, usually £2, and maintenance, usually at 1s 6d a week, unless he was well to do, in which case it could rise to 4s (the sums do not straightforwardly translate, but it was fairly adequate to provide for the baby and the basic payment was a quarter of the sum earned by a farm labourer).

The record of this may be among parish Overseers' papers in the county archives, or an alternative source is the order book of the magistrates at quarter sessions (also in the archives).

Some men paid up before being taken to court, in which case, if they handed a lump sum of about £40 to the Overseers (which covered maintenance until the child was 14), there may be a note of this: 'From Mr De Blank, about the lying-in of Ann Brown' in the Overseers' accounts. If the money was given directly to the girl, there will be no record, unless in the parish register, where before about 1850 the father may be named, even with some slight censure implied: 'the seventh child of My Lord Sandwich and Martha Ray of this parish'. If the child is stated to be 'reputed son of John Black', then everyone knows he is. If he is 'imputed son', then the girl says so, but he denies it, though the vicar is certain enough to enter it. Other terms which may be found are 'baseborn', 'spurious', 'misbegotten' or 'natural'.

Some earlier fathers were quite proud of their sons, or of their whole score-sheet. The great admiral Thomas Cochrane, Lord Dundonald, had a wife in every port and several inland as well, and cheerfully admitted to paternity. Some years later, he went round checking that each child was properly entered in the registers and corrected the spelling of his name from Cockram in one case.

Beware of the naming of foundlings at Captain Coram's Hospital in London. At first, they were named in rotation after the governors, but as they grew, people assumed these men were their fathers, so the practice was stopped.

Royal bastards generally did rather well, as witness the dukedoms listed in Chapter 5. The Hanoverian kings were cheaper, either handing out money and ignoring their offspring afterwards, or in the case of the Duke of Clarence, who became William IV, giving a mere earldom to the eldest son.

Royals and aristocrats

FITZCLARENCE

As Duke of Clarence, William was always strapped for cash, and thought he was doing rather well when he found a mistress who was also a meal-ticket. Dorothea Jordan was a talented actress, always in demand, and she financed their home by working on the stage, even when she was heavily pregnant from 1790 onwards with one or the other of their ten or eleven children, who were acknowledged and known as Fitzclarence.

Then the heiress to the throne, his niece Princess Charlotte, died in childbirth and it was hinted that if her uncles married, they would get money from Parliament. Faced by huge debts, William dumped the ageing Dorothea and married little Princess Adelaide of Saxe-Meiningen in 1818. She had two baby girls who both died, but no replacement for the strapping four Fitzclarence boys.

When he became king in 1831 William passed on one of his minor titles, Earl of Munster, to the eldest son, George, and gave the other sons honorary titles of Lord, as if they had been sons of a marquess; the daughters became Lady, except

WHAT IF THE CONNECTION IS ILLEGITIMATE?

Dorothea Jordan with one of the children she bore to William IV

the two of them who already had by marriage titles of their own as Countess of Erroll and Viscountess Falkland. Lord Frederick became a Lieutenant General, Lord Adolphus a Rear Admiral and the Rev. Lord Augustus eventually chaplain to Queen Victoria, who had succeeded his father as queen and saw nothing wrong, then, with illegitimate cousins. The Earl of Erroll was Hereditary High Constable of Scotland, first subject in precedence in Scotland after the monarch, and officiated when George IV, his wife's uncle, visited Edinburgh. Other daughters married well, Lady Sophia to Lord De Lisle and Dudley, Lady Augusta to the Hon. John Erskine, son of the Earl of Cassilis (later Marquess of Ailsa), Lady Mary to General Fox.

The Earl of Munster had married Miss Wyndham, illegitimate daughter of Lord Egremont, and his title went down four generations before reverting to a junior line.

ARE WE RELATED?

Elizabeth Milbanke, Viscountess Melbourne

WYNDHAM

The Earl of Egremont was a strikingly handsome man, who cut a swathe across society in George III's times. And in those days, court ladies (like the gentlemen) were not averse to having moderately public affairs. Their marriages were arranged by their fathers on a sort of treaty basis, owing little or nothing to love or even, at times, liking. It was accepted, even by the husbands, that as long as the wife provided the traditional 'heir and a spare', she could then go her own way, and any later children would be brought up in the family (just as his own children were brought up by someone else's family). The attitude persisted and only better contraception lessened the number of cuckoos in the nest.

WHAT IF THE CONNECTION IS ILLEGITIMATE?

Willliam Lamb, aged about 35

One of his early conquests was Lady Elizabeth Lamb. She, as Elizabeth Milbanke, married a complete boor, wealthy Peniston Lamb, and had produced the required heir, Peniston Jnr., but then jibbed and they lived separate lives. Lady Betsy fell for William Wyndham in a big way, and the result was her next son, William (and possibly another, Frederick); she then moved on to other lovers including George, the Prince of Wales, by whom she had a daughter, Emily. She got her husband appointed Gentleman of the Bedchamber as a joke, and created Viscount Melbourne.

There would have been no problem, but the younger Peniston Lamb died, and his brother William, every day looking more like Egremont, was now heir to the viscounty. When he went into Parliament, numerous people remarked what a remarkable resemblance he bore to his father – and they didn't mean Lamb. In 1805 he married Lady Caroline Ponsonby, daughter of the Earl of Bessborough

George, 3rd Earl of Egremont

WHAT IF THE CONNECTION IS ILLEGITIMATE?

(whose mother was another of the Prince Regent's ladies). She was a violent and unbalanced woman, who conceived a dreadful passion for Lord Byron. Willing as he was to accept most offers, Byron saw that Caro Lamb was nothing but trouble, and rejected her, in a series of cutting letters. She then turned on the world, and her unfortunate husband, writing a novel called *Glenarvon* which was full of thinly disguised characters, including Byron, the Duchess of Devonshire, Lady Jersey, and her mother in law, Lady Betsy. Her husband, though she could not fault his politeness and patience, was attacked for not fighting a duel with Byron. She even quoted Byron's letters rejecting her offers. The Lambs were embarrassed and Emily Cowper, William's sister, fell ill with anxiety. The Prince Regent (later George IV) remained a friend of Betsy's and reminisced with her daughter (and his), Lady Cowper, about holding her hand as she died. The only snag was that he had not been near her at any time in her last illness.

Lord Egremont used to keep a gallery with many portraits of ladies, and the gossip writer Thomas Creevey considers that they were all former conquests of his. In his old age, he took young Lord Sefton round the gallery, pointing out slyly a painting of his mother *and* his grandmother, remarried (three weeks after the death of her husband, Lord Craven) to the Margrave of Brandenburg, both of whom Creevey thought were Egremont's conquests, and of Berkeley Craven – 'one of his stud', youngest son of the grandmother. Creevey himself was the illegitimate son of the previous Lord Sefton, so he knew the score.

There were other children of Lord Egremont – not by his wife, but by various other ladies. When he died, his title lapsed, after a short spell with a nephew. However, when the nephew died, the next real heir was George Wyndham, politely called the 'adopted' son of Lord Egremont, who had left him Petworth House and other property. He was created Lord Leconfield, and used the arms which the Earl had borne, in a border to show illegitimacy. The title was finally made up in 1963 to Baron Egremont.

The Wyndhams take their name from Wymondham, Norfolk (pronounced Windham), and one of them married the heiress of an estate at Orchard, Somerset, in the time of Edward VI. John Wyndham of Orchard Wyndham was the ancestor of Lord Egremont, his brother of Caroline Wyndham, heiress, who married William Quinn, later Wyndham-Quinn and Earl of Dunraven. There were ample Wyndhams of Dinton, Wiltshire, and Campbell-Wyndhams of Salisbury and Corhampton, Hampshire, as well as some who returned to Norfolk.

ARE WE RELATED?

Cavendish

In the 18th century, more or less all the aristocratic families seemed to have produced some illegitimate children. The *ménage à trois* of William, 5th Duke of Devonshire, his feather-brained wife Georgiana (Spencer) and his mistress, Lady Elizabeth Foster, was constantly added to by one or the other. The illegitimate children were Charlotte Williams (his by Charlotte Spencer, a milliner), Caroline St Jules (Bess's), Augustus Clifford (Bess's), Eliza Courtney (Georgiana's by Charles Grey MP), three legitimate Cavendish children and two possibly legitimate Foster children. Caroline St Jules married Lady Betsy Lamb's fourth bastard, George, who possibly was not the son of the Prince. Charlotte Williams married the nephew of the land agent Thomas Heaton.

Maitland

In the Scottish system there is a provision for 'handfast marriages', which meant that if you took hands publicly and announced your intention to marry, you were married, or if you lived together as man and wife, this counted as a marriage. There was a provision for registering these marriages officially, however much later. This applied to ordinary folk, but not normally at all for the inheritance of peerages. However, if you have a good lawyer, you can get away with almost anything.

Charles Maitland, 6th Earl of Lauderdale, had six sons, and his heir, the 7th Earl, had four, so the pickings for the younger sons in Scotland seemed slim. The 8th Earl had two sons, and although both succeeded him, neither had children, so the title devolved on their first cousin, only remaining grandson of the 7th Earl whose only son died as a small child. The title in 1878 therefore reverted to the line of the second son of the 6th Earl, who had taken the name Barclay-Maitland. This 12th Earl was unmarried and died six years later.

Now things got interesting. The third son of the 6th Earl was a soldier, served at the Siege of Quebec, was deputy adjutant general in Canada and then moved on to America, where he was promoted to colonel. He liked the place, so he stayed on and set up home with a widow lady, Mrs McAdam, as housekeeper. Before many years had passed, she was the mother of three sons by him, and another on the way. In 1772, he fell ill, knew he was dying and decided to make things right by marrying her, which he did on 11 July, before he died on 13 July. He made his will too, leaving money to her and to his 'natural sons known as

Maitland', which clearly meant illegitimate. The oldest and youngest sons went into the army, and both died without issue. The third son joined the navy, became an admiral, married twice but died childless.

The second son, Patrick, went into a bank in Calcutta, did rather well and went back to Scotland, to live in Kilmaron Castle. He was not expecting anything, since there were still five people (and more potentially) between him and the title. He died in 1821, and his elder son in 1878, leaving two sons, Frederick and George.

In 1884, the 12th Earl died and suddenly the opportunity presented itself. Frederick claimed the title, and just possibly may not have realised that his great-grandfather was illegitimate. Frederick had been a soldier but had then served for some years in the foreign department of the Government of India, so he was presumably used to paperwork.

However, the next male heir did know, or suspected. He was descended from the fifth son of the 6th Earl, Frederick Lewis, who married the heiress of Makgill, and adopted the additional names Makgill-Crichton. His senior descendant now was his great-grandson, David Maitland-Makgill-Crichton of Rankeillour, a young soldier, who claimed the earldom.

There is no doubt that Richard Maitland considered his sons illegitimate, but unless the Makgill lawyers got hold of that will, they wouldn't be able to show this damning piece of evidence. They evidently were not as sharp as Frederick's men and possibly did not realise the claim would be proved in England. The marriage was in America and it was difficult to access details, or they may have decided that handfasting applied, or that there had been a previous ceremony. Frederick was given the benefit of the doubt and adjudged 13th Earl, against all the legalities of the case, and the line from him continues, with one male per generation. The unfortunate Maitland-Makgill-Crichtons did not even get a consolation prize of a barony. They are undoubted next heirs (with numerous males) if anything happens to the descendants of Frederick. The Earl a decade ago was well aware of the situation and thought it great fun.

If your claim is through an illegitimate son, you are very unlikely indeed to do as well, even if you have sharp lawyers, since so will the other side. The family connection by blood, nevertheless, may exist, if you can prove it is more than just family rumour.

CHAPTER 10

TRACING YOUR OWN ANCESTORS

In every case, the first step is to ask the family what they know already, then to check the information for accuracy in official records. It isn't that they tell you lies, but they may not know every last name and date correctly, working from memory of what someone has told them. Always work back from what you know to what you don't know, never downwards from an ancestor you would like to own.

If your ancestors were in the UK after 1837 (for England and Wales), then checking will involve using the General Register Office (GRO) indexes of births, marriages and deaths, which are accessible either in London at the Family Records Centre (FRC) in Islington or in the major reference libraries of most counties and large cities (both of these are normally complete from 1837 onwards); the indexes are also available in some family history society research rooms overseas, which may have a less than complete set. You can also get access to these indexes through any Church of Latter-day Saints (LDS) family history centre worldwide, where a certain number of years may be kept in stock, but more often you will have to order the films of sections from their central distribution centre in Salt Lake City. (Sometimes they are known overseas as 'St Catherine's Indexes', from the place where they used to be kept four or so years ago.)

If you locate a birth date you are sure of, then you can send for the certificate, which will show the names of both parents, including the maiden name of the mother; this enables you, working back from the birth date, to find the marriage of the couple. That certificate will show their ages and the names of their fathers, which should lead to their own birth certificates, and so on.

Older English and Welsh death certificates do not show the names of parents, or birthplaces, marital details, etc. What you get in a death certificate is:

- *for a male adult or unmarried female* the names, the date and place of death, the age, the occupation, the cause of death (and duration of illnesses) and the name and address of the informant, who may be a relative

- *for a married woman or widow* the above information with the name of the husband as 'occupation'

- *for a child* the above details, with the name of the father and his occupation.

English and Welsh birth or death certificates cost £6.50 (2002) and can normally be obtained from a *local* registrar, in the area shown in the indexes, or by ordering, personally or through an agent, at the FRC. Marriage certificates, which are filed differently locally and much less accessibly, in a separate place for every church or chapel, normally should be bought centrally (unless you know which actual church was used). These certificates, and any others you wish to buy, can be ordered from the central agency, ONS, PO Box 2, Southport, Merseyside PR8 2JD, or with credit cards, on-line at <certificateservices@ons.gov.uk> or by phone, 0151 471 4800. With the reference data obtained from the GRO indexes (year, quarter, district, alpha-numerical group) a certificate will cost £8: without it, if you know the year or even the exact date, it costs £11, and unless you have very close identifying information, they will not search at all. If you don't know at least the year, date and place, especially if the name is not an uncommon one, it would be best (and cheapest) to use an agent who works in London.

Only a small amount of this index information is available on-line. A group of volunteers have extracted (so far) about 25 per cent of the indexed names and placed them on the <FreeBMD@rootsweb.com> site. This information is also available through the commercial Ancestry.com site (and by agreement must be free even there), though several errors have been introduced by Ancestry in names of districts (Richmond-on-Thames, Surrey, is called Richmond, Yorkshire, for example). The whole of the births, marriages, deaths indexes for Cheshire are on-line. You still have to order the certificates, in either case, and no information from certificate registers is freely given at the moment.

If your ancestors are Scottish, then the certificate information does not start until 1855, but the detail is better. A birth certificate will give the date and place of marriage; a marriage certificate names both parents of the couple, not just the father. A death certificate gives the names of both parents of the deceased, even for an elderly person, and whether they are dead or alive. That is, of course, if the person notifying knows this, which may not be the case if someone dies aged and alone. The 1855 certificates contain extra information even to that. Scottish information in index form is on-line for years up to 1890 (later to 1920s) on the www.origins.net/gros site. This is accessible for a fee of £6 for 24 hours' continuous use, so plan your searches very carefully in advance, or the fee will run out before you have finished thinking about it. You still have to order the certificates from Edinburgh, at a cost of £10 each. The IGI contains a considerable amount of information from these GROS indexes for the years 1855 – 75, in index form, and the LDS centres have or can get the indexes in microfiche form at least to 1920.

Irish civil registration did not start until 1864, though there are records of Protestant (or mixed) marriages from 1845. A limited amount of this civil information is included in the IGI; certificate information is on the English pattern. Certificates cost less than English ones (£5).

If you can get positive family information of a name existing in 1901, you can access the census for that year on-line at <www.census.pro.gov.uk/>. The index of names, with just enough identifying information, of age, occupation, birthplace and census place, is free, then you pay 75p to see the image of the entry, or 50p to see a transcription of it. The indexing has been done in too little time, and therefore may well be faulty, so you will need to think up all possible variations under which the name could appear. If you are experienced with computer databases, you will be able to use 'wild cards'. Select parts of the name that are unlikely to change and replace the rest with an asterisk. If you are looking for Frederick Randall, it could appear as Randall, Randell, Randle, Randale, etc. Frederick Rand* would get all of these. You might need to allow for Rendall, Rendle, Rundall, etc. too, which would turn up if you used a second wild card. The payment for the viewing of the census is by credit card (with a minimum cost of £5 for a period of 48 hours); or by a £5 voucher, which lasts for multiple use over six months.

If you know that someone was alive in early 1881, there is a full transcription of the census for that year available either on microfiches for individual counties or on a CD-ROM covering the whole of England, Wales and Scotland. The transcription was made by family historians all over the UK, and although it is by no means perfect, it is an improvement on the 1901 index. The results were keyed in (not always correctly) and the work processed by Americans and the resulting 26-disk CD is sold by the Church of Jesus Christ of Latter-day Saints at cost (£29.95 in the UK, and about $30 in the USA, also available locally in Australia and New Zealand).

This also provides an alphabetical index, with name, surname, approximate date of birth, county of birth and census county. In the index, you select a likely entry, and click on it, which prompts you to insert one of the regional disks. The groupings of counties are somewhat peculiar. Buckinghamshire, very much to the west of London, is grouped as 'Greater London East', for instance. Entries for Sunderland, in the north-east of England, are confused with those for Sutherland, in the north of Scotland.

In the regional disks you can use wild cards and double forenames. The list of entries corresponding to what you have requested will show in the top half of the screen, and as you move down the list, the corresponding fully transcribed entry for that person's whole household will appear in the bottom half of the screen. You can also view the 'neighbours' of that household, which may reveal other members of the family in the same street.

This CD-ROM is an ideal way of locating a family when you only have sketchy information about their names and where they lived before emigrating in the 1890s or early 1900s. It is useful to use it before you embark on the more complicated and protracted hunt through the GRO indexes of births, etc.

A census entry shows the name, age, relationship to the head of the household, occupation and birthplace for everyone. Armed with this information, you can get further back.

The *occupation* will suggest whether it is worth looking for a will or not. All wills indexes for England and Wales from 1857 to 1943 are available on microfiche in archives or major reference libraries of every county in the UK, and also through LDS family history centres worldwide. The indexes are very detailed and enable you to build up a skeleton pedigree of the senior members of the family. LDS have also filmed these wills, though access is not so simple.

After 1943, the only access to indexes of wills is at First Avenue House, High Holborn, London, where seeing a fax of the will (after a delay) costs £5. You can also order a copy of any English or Welsh proved will from 1858 to date from the District Probate Registry, Duncmbe Place, York YO1 7EA, or from any District Probate Registry, see phone book, fee £5. If you can state (from the indexes) which court proved the will, it will speed things up, but providing the name, year of death and location will do. If you are seeking 'John Smith of London, roughly 1875', you will need to supply an address, a district at least, and the names of widow and son/s, since there could be several John Smiths.

The *birthplace* will lead you into the location of events before 1837, which is essential before you can find the family in parish registers. These are almost all now deposited not in the parish church, but in the archives of the county concerned. In a city, there may be a number of different parishes anyway. Very many but by no means all of the parish registers of England, Wales and Scotland have been filmed by the LDS and are available on loan at their family history centres.

If you are uncertain which parish in a city (especially London) is involved, the quickest way to check may be the IGI. If a parish's records have been filmed and controlled extraction of the events made, there will be a basic index which may show a likely name. It is totally unsafe to build a pedigree on the IGI alone, since the grandpa you choose may have died at the age of eleven, but it is a useful pointer to where to look in the registers. As I mentioned above, any entries labelled 'relative' or dated 'ab(ou)t 1750' are only guesses and should be treated with suspicion until checked.

Work backwards in the parish registers, and note down all siblings of your likely ancestor and all events to people of the surname (not ignoring the female lines). If your family rumour says you are 'connected' with the noble family of Bloggs, then what you are hoping to find is some evidence that your own ancestors get 'better' as they go back in time.

The fact that they turn out to be agricultural labourers in 1851 is not an absolute bar. A lot of farmers had to sell up in the difficult 1830s and 1940s. The general rule of inheritance in England is by primogeniture, meaning that the eldest son gets the lot, or at least the best of any land or business, or most of the money. Younger sons, even of gentlemen, were put into a trade or profession which gave them the chance of making money of their own, and then it was up to them. Some did so well that they overtook the senior branch of the family in wealth, land and even titles, but the tendency was for the eldest son of the eldest son to get richer, while the youngest son of the youngest son got poorer.

The knowledge of a connection could persist even through the centuries, though the financial status and even the spelling of the name did not. Sometimes the former glory was remembered in the parish. For instance, a Sussex vicar noted, against the burial of a pauper named Mowcumber, from the Workhouse: 'he was of the family of the Montgomeries, once lords of this place'.

ROBINSON

The family may hold on to this memory too. Some years ago, I taught family history to an elderly man whose aunt had informed him he ought to be the Earl of Ripon. He was a company director and his father an eminent civil servant, so there might have been something in it. But two generations back, his ancestor proved to be a watchmaker in Sheffield. At least the county was right, but Robinson is a very common name.

However, the printed pedigree of the Earls of Ripon, who became marquesses, showed beyond a doubt that they had died out for want of male heirs, and all the younger generations who might have had a claim are very well documented. The landed estate of Studley Royal went to the heirs of a niece, who married Henry Vyner of Gautby.

The Robinsons were originally a comfortable merchanting family in the City of York, settling in the Thirsk area of Yorkshire. The senior line did pretty well, went into diplomacy, then politics, and one became Prime Minister (though not exactly a distinguished one, known from his naively optimistic attitude as 'Prosperity Robinson'). They held titles of Lord Grantham (1761), Viscount Goderich (1827), Earl de Grey (1813), Earl of Ripon (1833) and Marquess (1871), but there are no male Robinsons descended from the first or any ennobled member of the family at all. There is no claim to a title from the descendants even of the brothers of the first man who got it.

What did emerge was that the Sheffield watchmaker was born in a village near Thirsk, and that he was the youngest son of a farmer, whose ancestors got 'better' socially as they were pursued backwards, until in the 1600s they were referred to with the honorific prefix of 'Mr'. The connection of the comfortably off Mr Robinsons of Ripon and Thirsk with 'Mr' William Robinson two miles away is very likely, though it is not clear which 'cousin William' of three he is.

Whether the aunt had passed on a family tradition that her own ancestors were related to the Earl of Ripon, or whether, as an educated woman, she had

ARE WE RELATED?

read the obituaries of the last ennobled Robinsons, fallen a victim to romantic imaginings and hazarded a guess that, for once, was on target, we just don't know. She died long ago, never having researched personally, but convinced to the last that she was right. Other aunts may have the same deep and sincerely held convictions which simply don't stand up to investigation at all.

So if in your own searches you find your family described as farmers or yeomen, there is a reasonable chance of a link to a well-connected family. If, before 1800, they are called 'Mr' and the females 'Mrs' (which applied to married or unmarried ladies, even small girls, of good social level), then locally they were recognised as gentlemen or rich and important people.

If the family have land or money, then there are likely to be wills, which will mostly be either in the archives of the county concerned, or, in some cases, for the wealthier people, in the Public Record Office, since they were proved in the Prerogative Court of Canterbury. This was not based in Canterbury, Kent, but in London and had a whole organisation of lawyers dealing with wills. Most of these wills have been filmed and can be accessed through the LDS, but reading them, and making sense of them, can be quite complicated, until you have had practice in reading old writing and the jargon used.

Nevertheless, researching your true ancestry is the only way you can prove to others, but more importantly, to yourself, that you really are related.

Appendix: Family names of the peerage

A peerage volume is arranged by the name of the chief title, not the family surname, and some people own more than one title. For the record, the family names which are those of the nobility differing from their titles are as follows.

D = Duke; M = Marquess; E = Earl; V = Viscount; B = Baron; (ext.) = title extinct.

Acton (Lyon-Dalberg-): Acton B

Adderley: Norton B

Addington: Sidmouth V

Agar: Normanton E

Aitken: Beaverbrook B

Alexander: Caledon V; Cobham B

Allsop: Hindlip B

Aman: Marley B

Annesley : Valentia V

    Grove-Annesley Annesley E

Anson: Lichfield E; Anson V

Arden (Baillie-Hamilton-): Haddington E

Armstrong: (Watson-): Armstrong B

Arthur: Glenarthur B

Ashley-Cooper: Shaftesbury E; Ashley B

Asquith: Oxford and Asquith E

Astley: Hastings B

Bacon: (ext.) Verulam E

Bailey: Glanusk B

Baillie: Burton B

    Cochrane-Baillie: Lamington B

Baird: Stonehaven V

Baldwin: Baldwin of Bewdley E; Corvedale V

ARE WE RELATED?

Balfour: Kinross B; Riverdale B; Balfour of Inchrye B

Bampfylde: Poltimore B

Baring: Cromer E; Ashburton B; Northbrook B; Revelstoke B

Barnewall: Trimlestown B

Barrie: Abertay B

Bass: (formerly) Burton B

Bateson: (-de Yarburgh): Deramore B

Bathurst: Bathurst E; Bledisloe V; (ext.) Ranelagh E

Beach (Hicks-): St Aldwyn E

Beauclerk: St Albans D

Beaumont: Allendale V.; Beaumont B; (ext.) Earl of Leicester

Beckett: Grimthorpe B

Bellew: Bellew B

Benn: Stansgate V

Bennet: Tankerville E

Bentick (Cavendish-): Portland D; Titchfield M; Cirencester B; Bolsover B

Beresford: Waterford M; Decies B

Berkeley: Berkeley B; (ext.) Berkeley E

Bernard: Bandon E

Berry: Camrose V; Kemsley V

Bertie: Allington and Lindsay V; Bertie of Thame V

Best: Wynford B.

Bethell: Westbury B

Bethune, Lindsay- : Lindsay E

Betterton: Rushcliffe B

Bigge: (ext.) Stamfordham B

Bigham: Mersey V; Nairne B

Bingham: Lucan E; Bingham V; Clanmorris B

Blackwood (Hamilton-Temple-): Dufferin and Ava M

Bligh: Darnley E; Clifton B

Weld-**Blundell**, Manchester D; Yarborough E

Boot: Trent, *B*

Booth, Sclater- : Basing *B*

Borthwick: Whitburgh *B*

Boscawen: Falmouth *V*

Bourke: Mayo *E*

Bouverie:

    Pleydell-: Radnor *E*

    Utthwatt-: Utthwatt *B*

Bowes-Lyon: Strathmore and Kinghorn *E*; Lyon *V*; Glamis *B*

Bowyer: Benham *B*

Boyd: Kilmarnock *B*

Boyle: Cork and Orrery *E*; Shannon *E*; Glasgow *E*; Boyle *V*

Brabazon: Meath *E*

    Moore- : Brabazon of Tara *B*

Brand: Hampden *V*

Brett: Esher *V*

Bridgeman: Bradford *E*

Brodrick: Middleton *E*

Brooke: Alanbrooke *V*

Brooks: Crawshaw *B*

Brougham: Brougham and Vaux *B*

Broughton: Fairhaven *B*

Browne: Sligo *M*; Kenmare *E*; Oranmore and Browne *E*; Kilmaine *B*

Brownlow: Lurgan *B*

Bruce: Elgin and Kincardine *E*; Aberdare *B*; Bruce *B*; Balfour of Burleigh *B*

Brudenell: Cardigan *E*

    Brudenell-Bruce: Ailesbury *M*

Buchan: Tweedsmuir *B*

Buckley: Wrenbury *B*

Burns: Inverclyde *B*

Butler: Ormonde *M*; Carrick *E*; Lanesborough *E*; Mountgarret *V*; Dunboyne *B*

ARE WE RELATED?

Byng: Strafford *E*; Torrington *V*

Cadogan: Cadogan *E*; Chelsea *V*; Oakley *B*; Cadogan *B*

Nall-**Cain**: Brocket *B*

Cambridge: Athlone *E*; Cambridge *M*; Eltham *E*; Northallerton *V*

Campbell: Argyll *D*; Kintyre and Lorne *M*; Lochow *V*; Sundridge *V*; Breadalbane and
Holland *E*; Tay *V*; Glenorchy *B*; Cawdor *E*; Colgrain *B*; Glenavy *B*; Stratheden *B*;
Methuen-Campbell: Methuen *B*

Canning: Garvagh *B*

Capell: Essex *E*

Conolly-**Carew**: Carew *B*

Carleton: Dorchester, *B*

Carnegie: Northesk *E*; Southesk *V*; Fife *E*

Cary: Falkland *V*

Caulfeild: Charlemont *V*

Verney-**Cave**: Braye *B*

Cavendish: Devonshire *D*; Hartington *M*; Burlington *E*; Cavendish *B*; Chesham *B*;
Waterpark *B*

Cavendish-Bentinck: Portland *D* and *E*; Titchfield *M*; Woodstock *V*; Cirencester *B*;
Bolsover *B*

Cayzer: Rotherwick *B*

Cecil: Exeter *M* and *E*; Burghley *B*; Amherst of Hackney *B*; Rockley *B*

Cecil, Gascoyne: Salisbury *M*; Cecil of Chelwood *V*; Quickswood *B*

Chaloner: Gisborough *B*

Charteris: Wemyss and March *E*

Chichester: Donegal *M*; Templemore *B*

Childe-Villiers: Jersey *E*

Cholmondeley: Delamere *B*

Chubb: Hayter *B*

Spencer-**Churchill**: Marlborough *D*; Blandford *M*; Sunderland *E*; Spencer of
Wormleighton *B*; Churchill *B*

Churchman: Woodbridge *B*

Napier-**Clavering**: Napier and Ettrick *B*

Clements: Leitrim E

Clinton, Fiennes- , Pelham: Newcastle D; Lincoln E

Clive, Windsor- : Plymouth E

Coats: Glentanar B

Cochrane: Dundonald E

Cockayne: Cullen of Ashbourne B

Cocks: Somers B

Coke: Leicester E; Coke V

Cole: Enniskillen E; Cole V

Collier: Monkswell B

Colville: Clydesmuir B

Compton: Northampton M; Compton E

Cooper: Lucas of Crudwell B

    Ashley-Cooper: Shaftesbury E

Bewicke-**Copley**: Cromwell B

Corbett: Rowallan B

Corry, Lowry- : Belmore E

Cotton, Stapleton- : Combermere V

Courtenay: Devon E; Courtenay V

Money-**Coutts**: Latymer B

Craig: Craigavon V

Crichton: Erne E

    Crichton-Stuart: Bute M; Dumfries E

Cripps: Parmoor B

Crittall: Braintree B

Crossley: Somerleyton B

Cubbitt: Ashcombe B

Curzon: Howe E; Scarsdale V; Ravensdale B

Cust: Brownlow B

Dalrymple: Stair E and V

Darcy: (ext.) Holdernesse E; Darcy de Knayth B

ARE WE RELATED?

Davies: Darwen *B*

Davison: Broughshane *B*

Dawnay: Downe *V*

De Courcy: Kinsale *B*

De Grey: Walsingham *B*

De Montmorency: Mountmorres *V*

Denison: Londesborough *B*

Dent: Furnivall *B*

De Vere: Inchiquin *B*; (ext.) Oxford *E*

Devereux: Hereford *V*; (ext.) Essex *E*

Dewar: Forteviot *B*

Dixon: Glentoran *B*

Dodson: Monkbretton *B*

Douglas: Queensberry *M*; Drumlanrig *V*; Douglas (ext.) *E*; Morton *E*; Dalkeith (ext.) *B*; Angus (ext.) *E*

Drummond: Perth *E*; Strathallan *V*; Maderty *B*; Drummond *B*; (ext.) Melfort *E*; Perth *D*
Drummond-Hay: Kinnoull *E*

Dudley: (ext.) Leicester *E*

Duff: Fife (ext.) *E* and *D*

Duke: Merivale *B*

Duncombe: Feversham *E*

Dundas: Zetland *M*; Ronaldshay *E*; Dundas *B*; Melville *V*

Eaton: Cheylesmore *B*

Eden: Auckland *B*; Henley *B*

Edgcumbe: Mount Edgcumbe *E*

Edwardes: Kensington *B*

Egerton: Ellesmere *E*; Wilton *E*; Egerton of Tatton *B*

Eliot: St Germans *E*

Elliott: Minto *E*

Scott-**Ellis**: Howard de Walden *B*

Erskine: Mar and Kellie *E*; Erskine *B*; Buchan *E*

    St Clair-Erskine: Rosslyn *E*

    Kennedy-Erskine: Ailsa *M*

    Young-Erskine: Mar *E*

Evans: Mountevans *B*

Eyre-Monsell: Monsell *B*

Fane: Westmorland *E*; Burghersh *B*

Feilding: Denbigh *E*

Fellowes: Ailwyn *B*; De Ramsay *B*

Ferguson: Mar *E*

Fiennes, Twistleton-, Wykeham- : Saye and Sele *B*

Fitzalan-Howard: Norfolk *D*; Beaumont *B*; Fitzalan of Derwent *B*

Fitzclarence: Munster, *E*

Fitzgerald: Leinster *D*; Kildare *M* and *E*; Offaly *E*

Fitzherbert: Stafford *B*

Fitzmaurice: Orkney *E*

Fitzwygram: Wigram *B*

Fletcher: Winster *B*

Flower: Ashbrook *V*

Foley: Berkeley *B*

Foljambe: Liverpool *E*

Forbes: Granard *E*

Foster: Ilkeston *B*

Fox: (ext.) Holland *E*

    Lane-Fox: Bingley *E*

Fraser: Lovat *B*; Saltoun *B*

French: Ypres *E*; French *V*; De Freyne *B*

Ganzoni (Childs-): Belstead *B*

Gardner: (ext.) Burghclere *B*

Gibbs: Aldenham with Hunsdon *B*; Wrathall *B*

Gibson: Ashbourne *B*

ARE WE RELATED?

Gidley: Kilbracken *B*

Giffard: Halsbury *E*

Gilbey: Vaux of Harrowden *B*

Glyn: Wolverton *B*

Gordon: Aberdeen *M*; Huntly *M*

    Gordon-Lennox: Ricmond and Godon *D*

Gore: Arran *E*

    Gore Langton: Temple of Stowe *E*

Grenville: (ext.) Buckingham *D*, *M*; (ext.) Chandos *M*; (ext.)Temple *E*; (ext.) Cobham *B*; Kinloss *B*

    Morgan-Grenville: Kinloss *B*

Grey: Stamford *E*

Grigg: Altrincham *V*

Grimston: Verulam *E*

Grosvenor: Westminster *D*; Grosvenor *E*; Ebury *B*; Stalbridge *B*

Guest: Wimborne *V*

Guinness: Iveagh *E*; Moyne *B*

Gully: Selby *V*

Hamilton: Abercorn *D*; Boyne *V*; Hamilton of Dalzell *B*; Holmpatrick *B*;

    Cole-Hamilton: Enniskillen *E*

    Baillie-Hamilton: Haddington *E*

Hanbury-Tracy: Sudeley *B*

Handcock: Castlemaine *B*

Harcourt: Vernon *B*; ext. Harcourt *B*

Hare: Listowel *V*

Harris: Malmesbury *E*; FitzHarris *V*

Harmsworth: Rothermere *V*: Northcliffe *V*; Harmsworth *B*

Hastings: Huntingdon *E*

    Abney-Hastings: Loudon *E* and *V*

Finch-**Hatton**: Winchelsea and Nottingham *E*

Hay: Erroll E; Tweedale M
  Drummond-Hay: Kinnoull E
Heathcote-Drummond-Willoughby: Ancaster E; Willoughby de Eresby B; Aveland B
Henderson: Farringdon B
  Hobart- , Hampden- , (Mercer-) Buckinghamshire E
Hennessy: Windlesham B
Herbert: Carnarvon E; Powis E; Pembroke and Montgomery E: Darcy de Knayth B
Hervey: Bristol M; Bristol E; Jermyn E; Hervey of Ickworth B
Hoare: Templewood V
Hermon-**Hodge**: Wyfold B
Hogg: Hailsham V; Maghersmorne B
Holland: Rotherham V
Douglas-**Home**: Home E; Dunglass B; Douglas B
Hood: St Audries B
  Nelson-Hood: Bridport V
Hope: Linlithgow M; Hopetoun E; Aithrie V; Hope B
Hopwood: Southborough B
Howard: Norfolk D; Carlisle E; Effingham E; Suffolk and Berks E; Wicklow E; Strathcona and Mountroyal B; Howard of Penrith B; Howard of Glossop B
Hubbard: Addington B
Inskip: Caldecote V
Irby: Boston B
Douglas-**Irvine**: Queensberry M
Isaacs: Reading M; Erleigh V
Jackson: Allerton B
James: Northbourne B
Parker-**Jervis**: St Vincent V
Tuchet-**Jesson**: Audley B
Jocelyn: Roden E; Jocelyn V
Joynson-Hicks: Brentford V
Kearley: Devonport V

ARE WE RELATED?

Kemp: Rochdale *B*

Kennedy: Ailsa *M*; Cassilis *E*

Kenworthy: Strabolgi *V*

Keppel: Albemarle *E*

Kerr: Lothian *M*

   Ker-Innes: Roxburghe *D*

   Clark Kerr: Inverchapel *B*

King: Kingston *E*; Lovelace *E*

Kitson: Airedale *B*

Knatchbull: Brabourne *B*; Mountbatten *Countess*

Knox: Ranfurly *E*

Miller-**Lade**: Sondes *E*

Lamb: Rochester *B*

Lambton: Durham *E*; Lambton *V*

Lampson: Killearn *B*

Langdale: Mowbray, Segrave and Stourton *B*

Lascelles: Harewood *E*; Lascelles *V*

Law: Ellenborough *E*

Lawless: Cloncurry *B*

Lawson (ex Levy); Burnham *B*

Legge: Dartmouth *E*; Lewisham *V*

Gordon-**Lennox**: Richmond and Gordon *D*; Lennox *D*; March *E*; Settrington *B*; Kinrara *E*

Leslie: Rothes *E*

   Leslie Melville: Leven and Melville *E*

Lever: Leverhulme *V*

Leveson-Gower: Sutherland *D*; Stafford *M*; Sutherland *E*; Gower *E*; Trentham *V*; Strathnaver *B*

Lewin: Roberts *E*

Lewis: Essendon *B*; Merthyr *B*

Liddell: Ravensworth *E*

Lindsay: Crawford *E*; Balcarres *E*; Balniel *B*; Wigan *B*

Littleton: Hatherton B

Cunliffe-**Lister**: Swinton V

Lloyd: Mostyn B

    Lloyd-George: Lloyd George of Dwyfor E; Gwynedd V

Loder: Wakehurst B

Loftus: Ely M; Loftus V and B

Lopes: Roborough B

Lowther: Lonsdale E; Ullswater V

Lubbock: Avebury B

Lumley: Scarborough E; Lumley V

Lygon: Beauchamp E

Bowes-**Lyon**: Strathmore and Kinghorn E; Lyon V; Glamis B

Lyons: Ennisdale B

Lysaght: Lisle B

Lyttleton: Conham V; Lyttleton B; Westcote B

Blunt-**Lytton**: Lytton E

Maxwell-**Macdonald**: Ducie E

McDonnell: Antrim E; Dunluce V

Mackay: Inchcape E; Reay B

Mackenzie: Amulree B

    Blunt-Mackenzie: Cromartie E

    Montague- Stewart- Wortley- : Wharncliffe E

McLaren: Aberconway B

Macpherson: Stratcarron B

Maffey: Rugby B

Maitland: Lauderdale E; Maitland V; Lauderdale V; Boulton B; Thirlestane B

Henniker-**Major**: Henniker B

Samuel-**Mancroft**: Mancroft B

Manners: Rutland D; Granby M; Manners B; Roos B

Mansfield: Sandhurst B

Marquis: Woolton V

ARE WE RELATED?

Marsham: Romney *E*

Mason: Blackfield *B*

Massey: Clarina *B*

Maude: Hawarden *V*

Constable-**Maxwell**: Norfolk *D*

Monxwell: Farnham B

Meade: Clamwilliam *E*

Middleton: Norfolk *D*

Freeman-**Mitford**: Redesdale *B*

Molyneux: Sefton *E*, Molyneux *V*

Monckton: Galway *V*

Mond: Melchett B

Montague: Manchester *D*; Mandeville *V*; Montague *B*; Sandwich *E*; Swaythling *V*;
(ext.) Montagu *D*; Amwell *B*

    Montague-Douglas-Scott: Montague of Beaulieu

Montgomerie: Eglinton and Winton *E*; Seton *B*; Tranent *B*; Ardrossan *B*

Moore: Drogheda *E*; Moore *V* and *B*

Morgan: Tredegar *V*

    Morgan-Grenville: Kinloss *B*

    Deane-Morgan: Muskerry *B*

Hope-**Morley**: Hollenden *B*

Morris: Killanin *B*; Nuffield *B*

Mostyn: Vaux of Harrowden *B*

Mountbatten: Edinburgh *D*; Carisbrooke *M*; Milford Haven *M*; Mountbatten *E*

Muff: Calverley *B*

Mulholland: Dunleath *B*

Mullins: Ventry *B*

Munro: Alness *B*

Murray: Dunmore *E*; Mansfield *E*

Stewart-**Murray**: Atholl *D*; Tullibardine *M*; Strathtay *E*; Glenalmond *V*; Glenlyon *V*;
Strange of Knockyn *B*; Percy *B*; Murray *B*

Needham: Kilmorey *E*

Neville: Abergavenny *M*; Lewes *E*; Bergavenny *B*; (ext.) Warwick *E*

Nicolson: Carnock *B*

Nivison: Glendyne *B*

Noel: Gainsborough *E*

North: Guilford *E*

Norton: Grantley *B*; Rathcreedan *B*

Northcote: Iddesleigh *E*; St Cyres *V*

Nugent: Westmeath *E*

O'Brien: Inchquin *B*

Ogilvy: Airlie *E*; Ogilvie *V*

O'Grady: Guillamore *V*

Hughes-**Onslow**: Onslow *E*

Osborne: Leeds *D*; Carmarthen *M*; Danby *E*; Latimer *V*; Godolphin *B*; Osborne *B*

Paget: Anglesey *M*, Queenborough *B*

Pakenham: Longford *E*, Pakenham *V*

Pakington: Hampton *B*

Palmer: Selborne *E*; Rusholme *B*

Parker: Macclesfield *E*; Morley *B*

Parnell: Congleton *B*

Parsons: Rosse *E*

Partington: Doverdale *B*

Paulet: Winchester *M*; Wiltshire *E*; St John of Basing *B*; (ext.) Bolton *D*

Pearson: Cowdray *B*

Pease: Daryngton *B*; Gainford *B*; Wardington *B*

Pelham: Chichester *E*; Yarborough *E*;
    Pelham-Clinton: Newcastle *D*

Pellew: Exmouth *B*

Douglas-**Pennant**: Penrhyn *B*

Penny: Marchwood *V*

Pepys: Cottenham *E*

ARE WE RELATED?

Perceval: Egmont *E*

Percy: Northumberland *D*; Percy *E*; Beverley *E*; Warkworth *B*; Alnwick *B*;
      (ext.) Lovaine *B*; (ext.) Prudhoe *B*

Pery: Limerick *E*

Phillips: St Davids *V*

Phipps: Normanby *M*; Mulgrave *E*; Normanby *V*

Pickford: Sterndale *B*

Pierrepont: Manvers *B*

Pitt: (ext.) Chatham *E*

Pleydell-Bouverie: Radnor *E*

Plunkett: Fingall *E*; Dunsany *E*; Louth *B*

Pollock: Hanworth *B*

Pomeroy: Harberton *V*

Ponsonby: Bessborough *E*; De Maulay *B*; Sysonby *B*
   Talbot-Ponsonby: Shrewsbury *E*

Powell: Baden-Powell *B*

Orde-**Powlett:** Bolton *B*

Powys: Lilford *B*

Pratt: Camden *M*; Brecknock *E*; Bayham *V*; Camden *B*

Preston: Gormanston *V*

Primrose: Rosebery *E*; Dalmeny *V*; Primrose *B*

Prittle: Dunalley *B*

Ramsay: Dalhousie *E*

Ramsbotham: Soulbury *B*

Rhys: Dynevor *B*

Spring-**Rice:** Monteagle *B*

Richard: Milverton *B*

Roberts: Clwyd *B*

Robinson: (ext.) Ripon *M*; (ext.) de Grey *E*; (ext.) Rosmead *B*

Roche: Fermoy *B*

Rodd: Rennell *B*

Trevor-**Roper**: Teynham *B*

Rose: De Ros *B*

Rowley: Langford *B*

Rous: Stradbroke *E*

Russell: Bedford *D*; Tavistock *M*; Howland *B*; Russell *B*; Russell *E*; Amberley *V*;
　　　Ampthill *B*; De Clifford *B*; Russell of Killowen *B*; Russell of Liverpool *B*

　Hamilton-Russell: Boyne *V*

Hore-**Ruthven**: Ruthven *B*; Gowrie *E*

Ryder: Harrowby *E*

Sackville: De la Warr *E*

St Aubyn: St Levans *B*

St Clair-Stannard: Sinclair *B*

St John: Bolingbroke and St John *V*; St John of Bletsoe *B*

St Leger: Doneraile *V*

Samuel: Bearsted *V*

Sandilands: Torphichen *B*

Sausmarez: De Saumarez *B*

Savile: Mexborough *E*

　Lumley-Savile; Savile *B*

Scarlett: Abinger *B*

Sclater: Basing *B*

Scott: Eldon *E*

　Montague-Douglas-Scott: Buccleugh *D*

Seely: Mottistone *B*; Sherwood *B*

Forbes-**Sempill**: Sempill *B*

Seymour: Somerset *D*; Seymour *B*; (ext.) Seymour of Sudeley *B*; Hertford *M* and *E*,
　　　Yarmouth *E*; Beauchamp *V*; Conway *B*

Shaw: Craigmyle *B*

Shirley: Ferrers *E*; Tamworth *V*

Shore: Teignmouth *B*

Siddeley: Kenilworth *B*

ARE WE RELATED?

Sidney: De Lisle and Dudley V; (ext.) Leicester E

Sinclair: Caithness E; Pentland B;

Skeffington: Massareene and Ferrard V

Smith: Birkenhead E; Hambleden V; Bicester B; Carrington E; Colwyn B; Dudley B

Somerset: Beaufort D; Worcester M and E; Botetourt B; Hervert B; Raglan B

Spencer: Marlborough D; Blandford M; Sunderland E; Churchill B; Churchill V; Spencer E; Althorp V

Stanley: Derby E; Stanley B; Stanley of Alderley B

Stern: Michelham B

Stewart: Galloway E;

Strutt: Belper B; Rayleigh B

Stuart: Castle-Stewart E; Moray E

Sturt: Alington B

Sugden: St Leonards B

Talbot: Shrewsbury E; Talbot of Malahide B; Talbot of Chtewynd B

Taylor, Taylour: Headfort M

Temple-Gore-Langton: Temple of Stowe E; Temple E; (ext.) Palmerston V

Tennant: Glenconner B

Thelusson: Rendlesham B

Thesiger: Chelmsford B

Thynne: Bath M; Weymouth V

Graham-Toler: Norbury E

Townshend: (ext.) Townshend M;
   Townshend-Marsham: Romney E

Hanbury-Tracy: Sudeley B

Trench: Ashtown B
   Le Poer Trench: Clancarty B

Hill-Trevor: Trevor B

Turner, Turnour: Winterton E

Upton: Templetown V

Vane: Barnard *B*; (ext.) Cleveland *D*; (ext.) Darlington *E*
   Vane-Tempest-Stewart: Londonderry *M*
Vanneck: Huntingfield *B*
Vaughan: Lisburne *E*
Vereker: Gort *V*
Verney: Willoughby de Broke *B*
Vernon: Lyvedon *B*
Vesey: De Vesci *B*
Villiers: Clarendon *E*; Hyde *V*
Vivian: Swansea *B*; Vivian *B*
Waldegrave: Radstock *E*; Waldegrave *V*
Hope-**Wallace**: Linlithgow *M*
Wallop: Portsmouth *E*; Lymington *V*; Wallop *B*
Walrond: Walersan *B*
Walsh: Ormathwaite *B*
Ward: Bangor *V*: Dudley *E*; Ednam *V*; Ward *B*
Watson: Manton *B*; Thankerton *B*
Wauchope: Ventry *B*
Webster: (ext.) Alverton *V*
Weir: Inverforth *B*
Wellesley: Wellington *D*; Douro *M*; Mornington *E*; Wellesley *V*; (ext.) Wellesley *M*
Westenra: Rossmore *B*
White: Annaly *B*
Whiteley: Marshamley *B*
Wilbraham-Bootle: Skelmersdale *B*
Willey: Barnby *B*
Williamson: Forres *B*
Willoughby: Middleton *B* (ext.); Willoughby *B*
Wills: Dulverton *B*; (ext.) Winterstoke *B* (the tobacco family)
Wilson: Moran B; Nunburnhome *B*
   Tyrwhitt-Wilson; Berners *B*

ARE WE RELATED?

Wingfield: Powerscourt V
Winn: St Oswalds B; Headley B
Wodehouse: Kimberley B
Wood: Halifax E
Woodall: Uvedale B
Woodhouse: Terrington B
Wyndham: (ext.) Egremont E; Leconfield B; Egremont B
Yelverton: (ext.) Avonmore V
Yerburgh: Allworth B; Alvingham B
Yorke: Hardwicke E
Young: Kennet B

Bibliography

THE PEERAGE AND THE GENTRY

Burke's Commoners (well-to-do families without titles or large lands)

Burke's General Armory (coats of arms 'as used', not all properly granted)

Burke's Knightage

Burke's Landed Gentry (various editions: originally families with 1,000+ acres)

Burke's Peerage (many editions to 1976 – no connection other than the misuse of the trade name, with the modern Burke's Peerage Book of the Bloggs Family that has been exposed in most countries)

Burke's Vicissitudes of Families (aristocrats who had gone down in the world)

Complete Peerage (GEC[ockayne], V. Gibbs, etc)

Debrett's Peerage (much less detail on families other than living members)

Dictionary of National Biography (multi-volume, with supplements)

Encyclopedia Britannica (not latest editions)

Fairbairn's Book of Crests (helmet decoration used by armorial families and mottoes)

Fox-Davies' Heraldic Families (all authentically granted arms)

A Genealogical Guide (J. B. Whitmore 1903 – 53); The Genealogist's Guide (G. Marshall, 1903) The Genealogist's Guide (G. Barrow, 1975); and British Family Histories in Print (T. Thompson, 1980) (All listing any printed sources with pedigrees of three or more generations)

Genealogists' Magazine (series)

Miscellanea Genealogica (This and several other periodical surnames indexed by Stuart Raymond)

Musgrave's Obituaries (gentry to 1801)

Whitaker's Peerage, Baronetage, Knightage and Companionage (various dates)

Who's Who? (semi-annual); Who Was Who? (intermittent)

LOCAL TO MOST COUNTIES

County Record Society publications (local archive material)

Directories: Kelly; Pigot; Slater; White; and Post Office series (various dates 1800 to 1970s)

Extensive bibliographies for several counties published by Stuart Raymond

Heralds' Visitation Pedigrees (published for different counties, not entirely accurate)

Histories of the whole county or of places within the county: list from local libraries

Local learned or archaeological society publications

Modern Domesday (list of property owners of one plus acres, 1873 England and Scotland, 1876 Ireland – microfiche and CD versions)

Victoria County History (by parish, owners of manors, charities, etc)

ARE WE RELATED?

FAMILIES

Anderson, Louisa Garrett, Elizabeth Garrett Anderson (Faber 1939)

Brandon, Ruth, The Dollar Princesses (Weidenfeld & Nicholson 1980)

Cecil, Lord David, Young Melbourne (London 1939)

Creevy, Wm, Diaries

Elwin, Macolm, The Noels & The Milbankes (Macdonald 1967)

Fawcett, M. G., What I Remember (Fisher Unwin 1924)

Lovelace-Byron Papers MSS, Bodleian Library

Lovelace, Ralph Milbanke, Astarte: A Fragment of Truth (Scribner 1911)

Marchand, Leslie, Byron, A Biography, 3 vols. (Knopf 1961)

Martindale, Louisa, A Woman Surgeon (Gollancz 1951)

Palmer, Alan, George IV (Weidenfeld & Nicholson 1972)

Pankhurst, Sylvia, The Life of Emmeline Pankhurst (New York 1969)

Pankhurst, Sylvia, The Suffragette Movement (Longmans 1931)

Pearson, John, Stags and Serpents: The Cavendish Family

Prebble, The Highland Clearances (Secker & Warburg 1963)

Rodger, N. A. M., The Insatiable Earl (John Montagu, 4th Earl of Sandwich)

Romero, Patricia, Sylvia Pankhurst (Yale University Press 1990)

Tooley, Sarah, A., The Life of Florence Nightingale (Cassell 1910)

Walters John, Splendour & Scandal (Life in Bath) (Jarrolds 1968)

White, T. H., The Scandal Monger (Cape 1952)

Woodham-Smith, Cecil, Florence Nightingale (Constable 1950, many reprints)

Ziegler, Philip, Melbourne (Collins 1976)

Index

ARE WE RELATED?

ARE WE RELATED?